MEXICO

BY KATE CONLEY

Essential Library
An Imprint of Abdo Publishing
abdobooks.com

ABDOBOOKS.COM

Published by Abdo Publishing, a division of ABDO, PO Box 398166, Minneapolis, Minnesota 55439. Copyright © 2023 by Abdo Consulting Group, Inc. International copyrights reserved in all countries. No part of this book may be reproduced in any form without written permission from the publisher. Essential Library™ is a trademark and logo of Abdo Publishing.

Printed in the United States of America, North Mankato, Minnesota.
102022
012023

THIS BOOK CONTAINS RECYCLED MATERIALS

Cover Photos: Rubi Rodriguez Martinez/Shutterstock (San Miguel de Allende); Shutterstock (pattern)
Interior Photos: iStockphoto, 4–5; Shutterstock, 7, 8, 25, 30, 42, 57, 68–69, 78–79, 80, 83, 94; Prachaya Roekdeethaweesab/Shutterstock, 9; Iryna Kalamurza/Shutterstock, 11; Rex Wholster/Shutterstock, 14–15; Peter Hermes Furian/Shutterstock, 17 (Mexico); Web Tools/Shutterstock, 17 (globe); Marisol Rios Campuzano/Shutterstock, 19; Alex Bordeline/Shutterstock, 20; Nido Huebl/Shutterstock, 23; Fabrice Mieville/Shutterstock, 26–27; Nicks Image Stock/Shutterstock, 29; Mario Wong Pastor/Shutterstock, 31; THP Creative/Shutterstock, 32; Elzbieta Sekowska/Shutterstock, 35; Ethan Daniels/Shutterstock, 36; J. C. Gonram/Shutterstock, 38–39; Dmitry Rukhlenko/Shutterstock, 40; Ann Ronan Pictures/Print Collector/Hulton Archive/Getty Images, 43; Photo 12/Universal Images Group/Getty Images, 45; Everett Collection/Shutterstock, 46; Ritu Manoj Jethani/Shutterstock, 48; AP Images, 51; Pablo Martínez Monsiváis/AP Images, 53; Aleksandar Todorovic/Shutterstock, 54–55; Luis Barron/Eyepix Group/Future Publishing/Getty Images, 56, 72; Jon G. Fuller/VW Pics/AP Images, 58; Chad Zuber/Shutterstock, 61; Bisual Photo/Shutterstock, 63; Nelson Antoine/Shutterstock, 65; Olivier Laban-Mattei/AFP/Getty Images, 67; Artur Widak/NurPhoto/AP Images, 75; Jose Luis Magana/AP Images, 77; Mauricio Palos/Bloomberg/Getty Images, 81; Mauricio Palos/AFP/Getty Images, 85; Joseph Sorrentino/Shutterstock, 87; Fernando Llano/AP Images, 89; Kobby Dagan/Shutterstock, 90–91; Joe Raedle/Getty Images News/Getty Images, 92; Carlos Méjía Agencia El Universal/MAR/GDA/AP Images, 95; Eduardo Verdugo/AP Images, 96; Ramiro Reyna Jr./Shutterstock, 99; Gil C./Shutterstock, 101

Editor: Arnold Ringstad
Series Designer: Maggie Villaume

Library of Congress Control Number: 2022940385

PUBLISHER'S CATALOGING-IN-PUBLICATION DATA

Names: Conley, Kate, author.
Title: Mexico / by Kate Conley
Description: Minneapolis, Minnesota: Abdo Publishing, 2023 | Series: Essential Library of Countries | Includes online resources and index.
Identifiers: ISBN 9781532199479 (lib. bdg.) | ISBN 9781098274672 (ebook)
Subjects: LCSH: Mexico--Juvenile literature. | North America--Juvenile literature. | Latin America--Juvenile literature. | Mexico--History--Juvenile literature.
Classification: DDC 972.0--dc23

CONTENTS

CHAPTER ONE
A TOUR OF MEXICO 4

CHAPTER TWO
GEOGRAPHY 14

CHAPTER THREE
PLANTS AND ANIMALS 26

CHAPTER FOUR
HISTORY 38

CHAPTER FIVE
PEOPLE AND CULTURE 54

CHAPTER SIX
POLITICS 68

CHAPTER SEVEN
ECONOMICS 78

CHAPTER EIGHT
MEXICO TODAY 90

ESSENTIAL FACTS 100
GLOSSARY 102
ADDITIONAL RESOURCES 104
SOURCE NOTES 106
INDEX 110
ABOUT THE AUTHOR 112

CHAPTER ONE

A TOUR OF MEXICO

At just past seven o'clock in the morning, Ava's plane begins to descend. She can see the massive city below her, its streets forming a sprawling, grid-like pattern. Moments later, the landing gear lowers, and the plane glides onto the tarmac. Excitement wells up in Ava as she realizes they've finally made it to their destination: Mexico City, Mexico. Ava and her family collect their luggage and take a taxi to their hotel. After quickly freshening up, they are ready to begin exploring the city.

Ava's family is staying in the city's historic district. Most of the places they want to see are within walking distance. They start their morning by walking to a large

Seen from the air, the enormous sprawl of Mexico City extends as far as the horizon.

public square. Its official name is the Plaza de la Constitución, but most Mexicans refer to it as the Zócalo, which means "base" in Spanish. The Zócalo has been a major gathering place in Mexico City for generations. It is the largest public square in Latin America and one of the largest public squares in the world. Protests, concerts, fairs, parades, sporting events, and art shows all happen in the Zócalo. It is quiet this morning, though, as soldiers raise a massive Mexican flag high above the square.

Each side of the Zócalo is lined with historic buildings. The first stop for Ava's family is the National Palace, a huge structure that spans the Zócalo's entire east side. This site has been the headquarters of Mexico's government since the 1560s. Above the main door hangs a bell called the Campana de Dolores. Padre Miguel Hidalgo rang the bell in 1810, marking the start of Mexico's fight for independence from Spain. In modern Mexico, the president stands on a balcony above the bell on September 15, just before midnight. This tradition takes place on the eve of Mexico's independence day. The president cries out "¡Viva México!" to the crowd gathered in the Zócalo. It means "Long live Mexico!"

THE NATION'S CAPITAL

Mexico City is the capital of Mexico. More than 22 million people live there.[1] The areas surrounding the city are also well developed, and approximately a quarter of the country's population lives in and around Mexico City. It is one of the oldest continuously inhabited cities in the Americas. It is a lively, colorful city where ancient history and modern technology live side by side.

An enormous Mexican flag stands in the Zócalo, the large square at the heart of Mexico City.

The palace holds many important pieces of Mexico's history, but what Ava is most excited to see is its mural by famed Mexican artist Diego Rivera. As Ava approaches the grand staircase inside the palace, the mural comes into view. Its colors—bright blues, fiery yellows and oranges, dusty greens, and muted browns—draw her attention immediately. The sweeping mural covers the walls and tells the story of the country's history, from the early Aztec civilization to modern Mexico. The mural overflows with images of the nation's people, vividly bringing their story to life.

Elevated walkways allow visitors to safely explore the ruins of the Templo Mayor.

THE TEMPLO MAYOR AND A GODDESS

After finishing their tour of the palace, Ava and her family step out into the bright sunshine of the Zócalo. They begin the short walk to their next stop: the Templo Mayor. It is the site of the former Aztec city called Tenochtitlán. The area that is visible is the temple, which stood at the heart of the city. Though the temple is in ruins, Ava is fascinated by walking along its stone stairways and paths, imagining what life might have been like for an Aztec person living in the city.

UNEARTHING A SURPRISE

The ruins of Tenochtitlán and its Templo Mayor remained largely unknown until 1978. That year, workers installing electrical cables discovered the Coyolxauhqui Stone. Shortly afterward, scientists began excavating the site. They unearthed thousands of objects, many of which are now on display. The excavation work at the site is ongoing. In 2019, for example, scientists uncovered two sacrificial burial sites. This led to a renewed hope of finding tombs of Aztec royalty, which have remained hidden despite decades of excavation.

Once they've explored the site, Ava and her family go into the museum next to it. There, Ava learns why the Aztecs chose this location to build their city. They had received a message from the god of war and conquest, Huitzilopochtli. He told them to build the city where they found an eagle sitting on a cactus eating a snake. They saw it on this spot and began building the city there in 1325. By the time Spanish explorers arrived in 1519, more than 400,000 people lived in Tenochtitlán, making it the area's largest city.[2]

The museum has many artifacts from the Templo Mayor. Ava looks at the clay pots, masks, and figures that have been excavated from the site. What impresses Ava the most, though, is the Coyolxauhqui Stone. It is a massive, round stone spanning 11 feet (3.4 m) in diameter.[3] Aztec artisans carved it in about 1473 to commemorate the sacrifice of Coyolxauhqui, the Aztec goddess of the moon.

According to Aztec legends, Coyolxauhqui was angry with her mother, who had become pregnant. Coyolxauhqui planned to kill her mother. She sought the help of her 400 brothers, who were the stars in the sky. Before they could act, their mother gave birth to the god Huitzilopochtli. At his birth he was an adult, and he saved his mother before violently killing his sister. The Coyolxauhqui Stone represents this story and was placed at the bottom of Coyolxauhqui's temple as a reminder of her power.

DANCERS, LUNCH, AND A LEANING CHURCH

Ava and her family head back out to the Zócalo and begin strolling along the nearby streets. Smells from street vendors who have started cooking lunch on their large round griddles, called comales, reach Ava, and her mouth starts to water. She and her family walk until they find a vendor making *tlacoyos*. These are oval-shaped patties of corn masa, or dough, that are stuffed with fillings such as pork, cheese, or beans and then fried on a comal. They're hot, crispy, and delicious. She also tries an agua fresca, a fruit-flavored water.

As Ava's family eats, they can hear drums nearby. Once they've finished, they follow the music and find themselves back at the Zócalo. There they find a group of dancers known as *danzantes Aztecas* or *concheros*. The men and women wear traditional clothing, which includes feathered headdresses, loincloths, and face paint. While many tourists are drawn to the drums and dancing, the dances are not meant as entertainment. They are ways to connect with the past and honor the Aztec gods.

Traditional Aztec dances are often performed at seasonal festivals in Mexico.

When they've finished watching the dancers, Ava and her family walk to the north side of the Zócalo. There, they step into the cool, quiet darkness of the Catedral Metropolitana. This cathedral is one of Latin America's largest churches, and it took nearly 300 years to complete. Ava is struck by the ornate gold artwork throughout the cathedral, especially the Altar de los Reyes. It is a masterpiece made up of two massive paintings, several statues, and carvings of angels and saints.

As they head out, Ava notices a pendulum hanging from the ceiling of the cathedral. She asks her mom about it. Her mom tells her that the cathedral was built on top of a lake that was filled in hundreds of years ago. The unstable ground of the former lake, combined with earthquakes, has made the cathedral slowly and unevenly sink. The pendulum shows how much the cathedral is leaning. Ava notices that some of the walls lean too, and the floor slopes. At first this worries her, but her mom explains that engineers have worked to save the building and make it safe.

Ava's legs are getting tired. She's ready for a break, so her parents decide to hail a bright-green pedicab and hop into the back of it. The driver takes them on a scenic ride around the bustling

PARQUE ALAMEDA CENTRAL

The Parque Alameda Central was built on land that was originally an Aztec marketplace. After Spain conquered the Aztecs, the marketplace closed. In 1592, a Spanish official named Luis de Velasco turned the land into a park. The marshy areas surrounding the original marketplace were filled and planted with alamos, or poplar trees, which give the park its name. The Parque Alameda Central is the oldest public park in the Americas. Today it is still popular with locals and tourists alike, who enjoy the green space in the middle of the busy city.

streets of the historic district, ending at the Parque Alameda Central. It is a large park in the heart of Mexico City. They pay the driver and begin to explore the park, which is a shady oasis in the afternoon heat.

Eventually, they find a park bench and rest after their first day in Mexico City. It's been a busy day, and the family talks about all the sights they have seen. Ava's favorite has been the Templo Mayor. She is amazed at how the remains of an ancient city can exist right alongside modern buildings where people work every day. This mix of old and new is much like Mexico itself. It is a nation that has pride in its past, but one whose people are also looking forward and working to create a successful, strong nation for the future.

Despite travel restrictions from the COVID-19 pandemic, in 2020 Mexico was the third-most-visited country in the world. More than 25 million tourists traveled to Mexico that year.[4]

CHAPTER TWO

GEOGRAPHY

Mexico is in the southern part of North America. It is a large country that covers 758,449 square miles (1,964,375 sq km).[1] It is just less than three times the size of Texas, and it is the fifteenth-largest country in the world.

Mexico's neighbor to the north is the United States. A massive river forms almost two-thirds of the US-Mexico border. This river is known as the Rio Grande in the United States and as the Río Bravo del Norte in Mexico. To the south, Mexico borders Guatemala and Belize. Large bodies of water create Mexico's other borders. Western Mexico lies along the Pacific Ocean, while the eastern part of the country borders the Gulf of Mexico and the Caribbean Sea.

The Rio Grande stretches along much of Mexico's northern border with the United States.

The land in Mexico has amazing diversity, but one feature can be seen nearly everywhere: mountains. In northern Mexico, the Sierra Madre dominates the landscape. In Spanish, *Sierra Madre* means "Mother Mountain Range." The Sierra Madre is divided into three ranges. The Sierra Madre Occidental is in the west, the Sierra Madre Oriental is in the east, and the Sierra Madre del Sur is in the south. These three mountain ranges enclose the Mexican Plateau.

The Mexican Plateau, also known as the Mexican Altiplano, is a major landform in the center of the country. The northern part of the plateau is known as Mesa del Norte. This region is vast. It stretches from the border with the United States southward, reaching from Mexico's west to east coasts. The Mesa del Norte is dry and sparsely populated, and it rises to an altitude of approximately 4,000 feet (1,219 m) above sea level.[2] The southern part of the Mexican Plateau is called the Mesa Central. This region is wetter, more densely populated, and higher in elevation than the Mesa del Norte.

> ### THE RIO GRANDE
> At approximately 1,900 miles (3,060 km) in length, the Rio Grande is the fifth-longest river in North America. It begins as a snow-fed stream high in the Rocky Mountains of Colorado. From there, it flows south through New Mexico and then on to form the border between Texas and Mexico. Along its course, several other rivers empty into it. Depending on the time of year and local weather, the Rio Grande's conditions vary. In some places, the river is barely a trickle. In other places, it reaches depths of 60 feet (18 m).[3] The Rio Grande empties into the Gulf of Mexico near Brownsville, Texas.

MAP OF MEXICO

KEY:
- 🟥 Capital
- ⚪ City
- 📍 Point of Interest

NORTHERN MEXICO

The most prominent feature of northern Mexico is the Chihuahuan Desert, part of a belt of deserts stretching from Mexico up through the United States and Canada. It covers 250,000 square miles (647,500 sq km). More than 90 percent of the desert is in Mexico, while the remainder is across the border in the states of Arizona, New Mexico, and Texas.[4] This is the largest desert in North America. It has a high altitude, ranging from 3,000 to 5,000 feet (914–1,524 m). The altitude affects the climate. Daytime temperatures can reach 100 degrees Fahrenheit (38ºC), but they drop rapidly when the sun sets, making nights in the desert cool.[5]

Rivers and wind have carved canyons in the Sierra Madre Occidental. A series of five connected canyons, known as Barrancas del Cobre, or Copper Canyon, is one of the most scenic areas. It is located in the western part of northern Mexico. The canyon covers 25,000 square miles (65,000 sq km) and is deeper than the Grand Canyon.[6] The land is too rugged to travel by car, but a railroad nicknamed El Chepe brings visitors through the canyon. Among the many natural sites the train passes is the Cascada de Basaseachi, which is Mexico's tallest waterfall. It has an 804-foot (245 m) drop.[7]

Another prominent part of northern Mexico's land is the Baja California Peninsula. This narrow, mountainous strip of land extends 760 miles (1,223 km) southward from the US border. Baja has 2,038 miles (3,280 km) of coastline, and it is famous for its many beaches.[8] The Gulf of California separates Baja from Mexico's mainland. These warm, tropical waters provide many sheltered harbors.

A cable car system gives visitors unmatched views of the scenic Copper Canyon.

CENTRAL MEXICO

The state of Zacatecas serves as the border between the deserts of the north and the fertile land of central Mexico. This region is known as El Bajío. It is often considered Mexico's agricultural heartland because it has some of the nation's most fertile land. In addition, the region's land is rich in natural resources including silver, gold, tin, and copper. These metals have been mined from the land in El Bajío for centuries. Rich mines and fertile land have made El Bajío one of the most populated areas of Mexico.

Farmers grow corn and other crops in the rich farmland found in the state of Zacatecas.

Just east of El Bajío are upland valleys nestled within mountain ranges. People have lived in this area for thousands of years. It was once dotted with lakes, but most have been filled in over the years as more people settled the land. This area is home to Mexico City, which is the nation's capital and largest city. Mexico City was built on top of one of these lakes. Spanish conquerors drained Lake Texcoco after conquering the area in 1521. As a result, the land under Mexico City is unstable and is prone to sinking and other kinds of damage when earthquakes occur.

Mexico City's dense population combined with its location in a valley have also created problems. Scientists compare the valley where Mexico City is located to a bowl that has mountains for sides. Pollution generated by thousands of cars and businesses remains trapped in the bowl. When other factors—such as smoke from forest fires or a series of windless days—are added, the situation can get dire. In May 2019, Mexico City's officials declared a pollution emergency. They closed playgrounds and advised people to keep their windows closed because the air had become hazardous to breathe.

A SINKING CITY

Building their capital on top of a drained lake bed created unusual problems for the residents of Mexico City. The city is sinking at a rate of 20 inches (50 cm) per year, and scientists estimate this will continue for at least another 150 years.[9] The soil in the former lake bed under the city continues to slowly compact day after day, and the process cannot be reversed. The sinking does not happen evenly, which creates buildings that lean and floors that slope. It's a constant battle to prevent roads from cracking, buried pipes from breaking, and train lines from being damaged.

SOUTHERN MEXICO

To the southeast, Mexico contains an area known as the Yucatán Peninsula. In contrast to the northern deserts and upland valleys, most of the peninsula is low and lush. The Gulf of Mexico borders the west and north sides of the peninsula, while the Caribbean Sea forms its eastern shore.

These parts of Mexico are well known for their beaches and the excellent fishing. Tourists flock to this area, and some of its most popular sites are Cancún, Playa del Carmen, and Cozumel.

The land under the Yucatán Peninsula is made of limestone, which is highly porous. This part of Mexico gets a lot of rain, with some areas receiving about 80 inches (200 cm) each year.[10] The rainwater soaks into the porous limestone, and over time this has created a vast network of watery caves. Most of them are connected, forming a massive underground river network.

Access to the underground rivers is possible through a collection of 6,000 cenotes.[11] These are sinkholes in the limestone. In the past, the cenotes served as freshwater sources and religious sites for the Maya people who lived in the Yucatán. Today, many of the cenotes are open to snorkelers and divers who enjoy exploring the underwater caves, plants, and animals. One of the most impressive cenotes is Sac Actun, which leads to the world's longest underwater cave. The cave spans approximately 229 miles (368 km) before emptying its water into the Caribbean Sea.[12]

Mexico is home to 37 Holocene volcanoes.[13] Holocene volcanoes are those that have erupted in the past 12,000 years.

THE RING OF FIRE

Mexico lies along an area known to geologists as the Ring of Fire. It is a horseshoe-shaped belt that surrounds the Pacific Ocean's basin for 24,900 miles (40,000 km). Land along the Ring of Fire contains the meeting points of several tectonic plates. When the plates move, they can trigger

Tourists can descend into Sac Actun, which is found near the city of Tulum.

earthquakes and volcanic eruptions. The Ring of Fire is the site of 90 percent of the world's earthquakes and 75 percent of the world's volcanoes.[14]

Some of the volcanoes in Mexico are active, while others are dormant. The highest point in Mexico, known as Citlaltépetl Volcano, or Pico de Orizaba, is a dormant volcano. It reaches an altitude of 18,490 feet (5,636 m), and its last eruption occurred in 1687.[15] Two other well-known volcanoes in Mexico are Popocatépetl and Volcán de Colima. Popocatépetl, also known as Popo, is active. It began erupting in 1994, sending plumes of ash over nearby towns, and it has remained active since then. Volcán de Colima has been active since the 1500s. It has had multiple significant eruptions in the first few decades of the 2000s.

Earthquakes are also common in Mexico. Each year the nation has an average of 30,000 earthquakes.[16] Most are not dangerous, though the potential for disaster is always present. One of the nation's worst earthquakes occurred in 1985. At 7:19 a.m. on September 19, an earthquake measuring 8.1 on the Richter scale shook Michoacán. This state is along the Pacific Ocean,

A VOLCANO EMERGES

Mexico is home to one of the world's youngest volcanoes. A volcano now known as Paricutín arose in a field belonging to Dionisio Pulido. In February 1943, Pulido walked toward a deep depression in his field, and he noticed the earth there had split open. The area had experienced earthquakes for the past two weeks, but this was something different. Smoke arose from the crack, followed by the smell of sulfur. The ground rose and buckled, and later lava began to flow from the area. By the time Paricutín's eruptions stopped in 1952, it had formed a volcanic cone rising 1,391 feet (424 m) above the surrounding landscape.[17]

but the worst damage occurred approximately 200 miles (320 km) to the east, in Mexico City. The earthquake destroyed hundreds of buildings in the city, killed 10,000 people, and injured tens of thousands more.[18]

More recently, Mexico experienced two strong earthquakes within days of each other. On September 7, 2017, an earthquake measuring 8.1 on the Richter scale struck Mexico's southwest coast. The states of Chiapas and Oaxaca had the greatest damage, and the quake was felt by an estimated 50 million people in the region. Two weeks later, on the thirty-second anniversary of the devastating 1985 earthquake, another powerful earthquake shook Mexico.[19] This time it struck in central Mexico, near the city of Puebla. These frequent earthquakes are part of life for people in Mexico, as well as other countries along the Ring of Fire.

On a clear day, the volcano Popocatépetl can be seen from Mexico City.

CHAPTER THREE

PLANTS AND ANIMALS

From deserts to jungles, Mexico's land is home to an astounding variety of plants and animals. The landscape and climate determine what can thrive in each area. The hot, dry climate of northern Mexico and Baja can be harsh, but these areas still brim with life. The Chihuahuan Desert in northern Mexico is the most biologically diverse desert in the Western Hemisphere.

About 3,500 types of plants grow in the Chihuahuan Desert.[1] One of the most common of these is the creosote bush, which covers 40 percent of the desert.[2] It is a medium-sized plant, growing to an average size of four feet (1.2 m) tall.[3] The plant's

Mexico's arid regions are home to a diverse mix of hardy plant species, including cacti.

pointed, yellow-green leaves are thick and waxy to help it retain water, which lets it thrive in the desert's harsh conditions. When rain falls on the leaves, they release a strong scent that many people describe as earthy or musky.

The Chihuahuan Desert is also home to approximately one-quarter of the world's cactus species. They come in a variety of shapes and sizes. The prickly pear is one of the most recognizable cacti that is native to the Chihuahuan Desert. It grows in segments called pads, which are flat, broad, and oval-shaped. For years, people have used the prickly pear cactus for food. Its pads, often referred to as nopales, are served in salads, soups, and tacos. The fruit of the prickly pear can also be made into syrup, jelly, and candy.

In addition to plants, animals thrive in the Chihuahuan Desert. They take advantage of the many creosote bushes and are often found near them. Some, such as the black-tailed jackrabbit, eat the bush's leaves and seeds. Others, such as the desert tortoise, dig their nests under creosote bushes. The bushes' roots keep their nests stable, and the leaves provide a small amount of shade. Reptiles such as rattlesnakes, lizards, and geckos also use creosote bushes for nesting, shade, and cover from predators.

CREOSOTE TEA

Traditional healers in Mexico used the creosote bush to make medicinal tea. They steeped the branches and leaves in hot water for just seconds, producing a strong, bitter brew. Healers used the tea to treat a variety of diseases, including gallbladder stones, kidney stones, and cancer. The tea would also be applied directly to a person's body to treat fungal infections and ringworm. Some people still use creosote tea today, though its effectiveness has not been scientifically proven.

Desert tortoises emerge from their underground nests to feed and mate. They can live 50 to 80 years.

Larger animals also thrive in the desert, including mammals such as mule deer, pronghorn, foxes, and jaguars. Javelinas, which look much like wild boars, live there as well. Though not as common, grizzly bears, mountain lions, and gray wolves can also be found in this region. In addition, the desert supports more than 400 species of birds.[4] This includes birds that migrate from colder climates during the winter, as well as native birds such as roadrunners. Roadrunners can fly but more often run on the ground, reaching speeds of up to 20 miles per hour (32 kmh).[5]

Of the world's approximately 1,400 cactus species, 669 grow in Mexico, and 518 are native to the country.[6]

FORESTS

The plants and animals of the desert give way to a variety of forests that cover just over a third of Mexico's land.[7] Temperate forests are common in the Sierra Madre Occidental and Sierra Madre Oriental. Unlike the deserts, these areas are cool and wet. The temperatures average between 54 and 73 degrees Fahrenheit (12–23°C), and the annual rainfall is between 24 and 39 inches (60–100 cm).[8]

Mexico's temperate forests contain about 7,000 plant species.[9] The most common trees are pines and oaks. Other plant life includes a variety of grasses, ferns, myrtles, and mushrooms. The temperate forests host a variety of animal species as well. White-tailed deer, lynx, pumas, foxes, raccoons, rabbits, and squirrels are common mammals found in these ecosystems. Birds such as woodpeckers, red-tailed hawks, and golden eagles live there also.

Cloud forests are also found in central and southern parts of Mexico. These forests grow in areas with high humidity, heavy rainfall, and low clouds or fog. Pines, oaks, magnolias, ferns, and

> ### MONARCH BUTTERFLY BIOSPHERE RESERVE
> Every autumn, monarch butterflies migrate from the United States and Canada to the temperate forests of Mexico. The monarchs fly up to 2,800 miles (4,500 km) to reach the Monarch Butterfly Biosphere Reserve in central Mexico where they hibernate. Millions of monarchs crowd the reserve.[10] They come in such large numbers that branches sag under their weight, and clouds of orange and black fill the skies when the butterflies take flight.

To the ancient Maya and Aztec, the long, green tail feathers of the male resplendent quetzal represented the growth of plants in spring.

orchids live in these areas. Cloud forests support a wide variety of frogs and salamanders. Among the best-known birds in the cloud forests are the quetzals. They stand between 15 and 16 inches (38–41 cm) tall, and the bodies of some species are vibrant red, green, and blue. Male quetzals grow two tail feathers than can be up to three feet (1 m) long.[11] The ancient Maya and Aztec people considered the quetzal sacred.

DRY JUNGLES AND HUMID JUNGLES

Two types of jungles are common in Mexico: dry jungles and humid jungles. Dry jungles grow in western Mexico and in the northern parts of the Yucatán Peninsula. These areas have a distinct dry season and rainy season. Approximately 6,000 types of plants live in Mexico's dry jungles, most notably several kinds of palm trees and copal trees.[12] Animals in the dry jungles include anteaters, armadillos, weasels, mountain lions, jaguars, and coyotes.

Humid jungles—also referred to as tropical jungles—extend through eastern and southern Mexico, as well as the southern Yucatán Peninsula. These jungles receive steady rainfall all year, with an average of nearly 80 inches (200 cm) annually. The temperatures in humid jungles

Mexico's vast humid jungles feature distinct plant life at different levels above the ground.

DEFORESTATION

Mexico's forests have been threatened by decades of deforestation. The country's rates of deforestation are some of the highest in the world. Most of the deforestation has been caused by people clearing the land to use for growing crops and grazing livestock. The government has tried various programs to stop the deforestation, but it's still got a long way to go. Some programs, such as Sembrando Vida, have made the problem worse. This program pays people to replant trees. But in poor areas where people are desperate for money, they cut down healthy parts of the jungle so they can plant new trees and receive the payment, undermining the goal of the program.

are also steady, remaining above 64 degrees Fahrenheit (18°C) and rarely varying by more than a few degrees throughout the year.[13]

These conditions have created an environment that can sustain an amazing diversity of plants. The tallest trees, which can reach heights of 100 feet (30 m) or higher, form the canopy of the humid jungles.[14] Common trees in the canopy are mahogany, ceiba, and red cedar. Below the canopy, cacao trees, rubber trees, and soursop trees grow. The dense tree cover creates lots of shade near the jungle floor. Orchids, ferns, mosses, and lichens thrive in these conditions.

Mexico's lush, humid jungles teem with animals. Howler monkeys and spider monkeys live in the many jungle trees. The trees also provide a habitat for a variety of colorful birds, including the scarlet macaw, green parakeet, and royal toucan. Lower levels of the jungle are home to ground animals such as wild boars, anteaters, tapirs, otters, and raccoons. Many kinds of snakes, turtles, frogs, and iguanas also live in this habitat.

ALONG THE COASTS

Mexico's intertidal zones are the sandy, rocky areas between the ocean and land. The zones change throughout the day depending on the tides. When the tide is high, the zones are covered with water. When the tide is low, the zones are without water. Lichens and blue, green, and red algae commonly grow along Mexico's coastal rocks. Sea turtles, gulls, sandpipers, snails, and mollusks all live in the intertidal zones as well.

Mexico's vast shorelines are also home to mangrove forests. Mexico has more mangrove forests than nearly any other country in the world. Mangroves are trees and shrubs with parts of their roots exposed to the air. They thrive in poor soil that has high levels of salt and low levels of oxygen. Mangrove forests grow along the wetlands of the east and west coasts. These forests are not only beautiful but also helpful. The sections of their root systems that are underwater provide habitats for marine life, such as fish and crabs. The mangroves also control flooding, prevent erosion, and act as a natural filter for seawater.

Sand dunes are also part of Mexico's shorelines. They can be found in nearly all parts of Mexico that are along the coast. The dunes typically form behind beaches at the farthest point that the high tide can reach. Dunes are made of sand and organic materials, such as tiny bits of coral or shells. The shape of the sand dunes varies depending on the tides and the winds in each area. They can range from small, semicircular mounds to long belts that run parallel to the coastline. Sand dunes include a type of evergreen shrub called four-wing saltbush, an evergreen wildflower called

Mangrove trees cover about one-third of the Sian Ka'an Biosphere Reserve, located on the eastern coast of the Yucatán Peninsula.

The green moray eel is among the many species found along the Mesoamerican Reef.

sea purslane, sea grapes, beach vines, and silver palms. Insects such as beetles, flies, and wasps live in the dunes, along with larger animals such as turtles, herons, and frogs.

The waters off Mexico's shores also have amazing species in them. Kelp forests grow in the waters off the Pacific Coast of the Baja California Peninsula. Kelp is a kind of algae, and the variety of kelp that grows off Mexico's shores is giant. It can reach heights of almost 100 feet (30 m).[15] Unlike plants, kelp does not have roots. Instead, it attaches itself to rocks and gets all its nutrients from the ocean water. Kelp forests serve as a habitat and a food source for a variety of marine life, including sharks, fish, lobsters, and squid.

Just off the Yucatán coast is the Mesoamerican Reef. Located in the Caribbean Sea, it is the largest barrier reef in the Western Hemisphere. This type of reef is made of coral and runs parallel to the shore. At shallow points, the reef provides a barrier to the shore when hurricanes or other storms hit land, giving this type of reef its name. The Mesoamerican Reef begins at Mexico's Yucatán Peninsula and stretches for nearly 700 miles (1,127 km) along the coasts of Belize, Guatemala, and Honduras.[16] It is home to hundreds of kinds of fish and other types of sea life.

CHAPTER FOUR

HISTORY

People have been living in Mexico since about 9000 BCE. These early residents hunted and gathered plants, often moving seasonally in search of food. Gradually, the people of Mexico began to farm the land. Many of the native crops they grew, such as corn, avocados, and squash, are still familiar to people today. As farming practices improved, people no longer needed to move from place to place, and permanent settlements arose. These settlements produced Mexico's earliest society, the Olmec.

The Olmec settled in coastal lowlands near the present-day states of Veracruz and Tabasco. Their society reached its height between 1200 and 600 BCE. The Olmec culture remains largely unknown, though the evidence they left behind provides some clues.

The Olmec people left behind enormous carved stone heads.

The ruins of Teotihuacán feature enormous pyramids that visitors can climb.

Historians believe the Olmec were skilled artisans, built a large trading network, and worshipped many gods. The Olmec had a profound influence on later cultures in Mexico. For this reason, the Olmec are often referred to as Mexico's "mother culture."

The next major civilization in Mexico was made by the Teotihuacano people. Their society was complex and included farmers, merchants, artisans, and priests. They worshipped many gods, had their own writing system, and developed a large trading network. The society's capital city, Teotihuacán, was built approximately 30 miles (48 km) northeast of present-day Mexico City.

At its height around 500 CE, an estimated 200,000 people lived in Teotihuacán, making it one of the world's largest cities at the time.[1] It included apartments, canals, massive plazas, wide avenues, palaces, and temples. Ruins of the city still stand today.

The Maya people became the next major civilization to rule in what is now Mexico. They built their society in city-states across the Yucatán Peninsula, ruling the area from 250 to 900 CE. The Maya civilization developed a 365-day calendar similar to the one we use today and a writing system that used hieroglyphs. They farmed land using advanced techniques such as irrigation, and their deep understanding of mathematics and astronomy allowed them to predict solar and lunar eclipses accurately. One of Mexico's most famous remaining Maya sites is called Chichén Itzá. Its buildings include an observatory, temples, and ball courts. The Maya civilization fell in the 900s CE, and historians believe it was likely due to overpopulation.

ULAMA

The cultures of Mexican civilizations that existed before the land became a Spanish colony overlapped in many ways. A ball game called *ulama* is one of those ways. Originally called *ullamaliztli*, ulama has been played for 3,500 years, and approximately 2,000 ulama ball courts have been unearthed across Latin America. It is considered by many to be the world's oldest team sport. Three variations of the game still exist today. *Ulama de palo* is played with a ball and bat. *Ulama de brazo* is played with a one-pound (0.5 kg) ball that players strike with their forearms. *Ulama de cadera* is played with a heavy ball weighing up to nine pounds (4 kg), which players hit with their hips.[2] This game was popular in Maya and Aztec communities, as well as other native groups. Traditionally the game had connections to Indigenous gods and goddesses.

AZTEC CIVILIZATION AND SPANISH CONQUEST

The Aztec people created Mexico's last major Indigenous civilization. Around 1427, they joined forces with the remaining Maya and another powerful group called the Toltecs. Often called the triple alliance, this combination created an Aztec empire headquartered in the city of Tenochtitlán. The city was located on an island in Lake Texcoco, which is in present-day Mexico City.

Part of what made the Aztecs so powerful was their method of farming. They reclaimed lake beds and swampland, making them into raised fields and canals. This technique allowed crops to thrive, and the Aztec society grew quickly. The civilization they created was complex, with social structures influenced by earlier Indigenous peoples. Aztec society centered on religious beliefs. They worshipped a variety of gods through public rituals, some of which required human sacrifice.

At the civilization's height, Aztec leaders in Tenochtitlán governed between five and six million people in 500 city-states called calpulli.[3] The calpulli

A CACTUS, AN EAGLE, AND A SNAKE

According to Aztec legend, a god named Huitzilopochtli told the people to leave their homes. He told them to settle in the place where they saw an eagle sitting on a cactus eating a snake. The people wandered, seeking this place that Huitzilopochtli had instructed them to find. When they neared Lake Texcoco, they saw an island with an eagle on a cactus eating a snake. They stopped wandering and built the mighty city of Tenochtitlán on the island. The image of the eagle perched on a cactus eating a snake is on Mexico's national flag, reminding the people of their ancient history.

were independent, with each one having its own territory, leaders, military, schools, and temples. Ultimately, however, each one was still under the authority of Tenochtitlán.

In 1519, the Aztec leader Montezuma II faced a threat unlike any other in Aztec history. That year, Spaniard Hernán Cortés and an army of 500 landed in the present-day state of Veracruz.[4] According to the Aztec calendar, in 1519 the god Quetzalcóatl was meant to return. Montezuma heard reports about Cortés and wondered if he was Quetzalcóatl. Because of this, Montezuma invited Cortés to Tenochtitlán.

On the way there, Cortés encountered many Indigenous people who were unhappy with Aztec rule. He convinced them to join him, and the group heading to Tenochtitlán grew to include 6,000 local people. Cortés and his army attacked the city. After two years of fighting, Cortés and his army—which now included

A European illustration depicts the 1519 meeting between Cortés and Montezuma.

100,000 local allies—conquered Tenochtitlán in 1521.[5] Spanish forces continued to conquer other parts of Mexico as well. They claimed the land for Spain and created a colony called Nueva España, which means "New Spain."

NUEVA ESPAÑA

For the next 300 years, Nueva España was a Spanish colony. The Spanish created a new government system, provided land to colonists who arrived from Spain, and set up Catholic churches that converted millions of Indigenous people to Christianity. The conquest was disastrous for Mexico's Indigenous people. They lacked immunity to European diseases carried by the Spanish, such as measles and smallpox. Disease killed millions of people in Mexico. Those who survived the conquest and disease were often forced into slavery.

    Status in Nueva España was determined by a person's skin color and place of birth. Top status went to *peninsulares*. They were colonists who had been born in Spain, and they often held the highest, most powerful positions in the colony. The next highest status went to *criollos*. They were people of Spanish descent who had been born in Nueva España. Below them were the *mestizos*. They were people of mixed Indigenous and Spanish descent. At the bottom of the society were Indigenous people and enslaved people from Africa. The status lines were rigid and determined a person's future.

    Over time the criollos gained wealth and power, forming a growing segment of Nueva España's population. They resented the fact that they did not have as much power as the small group of peninsulares. As discontent spread, talk of a revolution grew. Spain's power over the colony weakened when French forces overtook Spain in 1808. On September 16, 1810, Catholic priest Miguel Hidalgo y Costilla issued a call for a rebellion from his town of Dolores. Now known as the Grito de Dolores, Hidalgo's call sparked the fight for independence. The war that resulted lasted a grueling 11 years, but on August 24, 1821, Nueva España gained its independence. The nation of Mexico was born.

THE EARLY REPUBLIC

Instability and war marked Mexico's early years as a republic. Between 1821 and 1860, Mexico's leader changed nearly 50 times.[6] And during these years, Mexico became involved in a conflict with the United States. It was known as the Mexican-American

Miguel Hidalgo y Costilla became a key figure in Mexico's struggle for independence.

An American illustration shows a major US victory in the Battle of Chapultepec in 1847.

War (1846–1848). The war centered on the newly independent nation of Texas. Texas had left Mexico and formed its own country in 1836. Mexican leaders refused to recognize Texas as an independent nation. They warned that if the United States annexed Texas, it would lead to a war.

In 1845, the United States annexed Texas. Relations between Mexico and the United States worsened quickly. On April 25, 1846, Mexican soldiers attacked American troops along the Rio Grande, leading to the start of the war. The war lasted nearly two years, ending with a US victory and the Treaty of Guadalupe Hidalgo on February 2, 1848. The war resulted in large territory losses for Mexico. This land would later form parts of the present-day states of Utah, Nevada, California, New Mexico, Arizona, Oklahoma, Colorado, and Wyoming.

> Mexico's territory losses following the Mexican-American War totaled more than 500,000 square miles (1,300,000 sq km).[7]

In January 1861, Mexicans elected Benito Juárez as president. He made several reforms to improve the country. Under the Juárez administration, school became mandatory, railways were built, and a rural police force was formed. Despite the reforms, trouble remained. When Juárez took office, the government was bankrupt. It could not repay loans it had taken from England, Spain, and France. In retaliation, each of these countries invaded Mexico. Ultimately France took control of the nation.

Though exiled, Juárez continued to actively resist French control of Mexico. On May 5, 1862, a small band of Mexican fighters defeated French forces at the Battle of Puebla. The battle became a symbol of Mexican power over foreign control. France finally withdrew its troops from Mexico in 1867.

The reforms Juárez started continued under Porfirio Díaz, who served as Mexico's president from 1877 to 1880 and again from 1884 to 1911. Under Díaz, the country continued to stabilize, but it came at a cost. Free elections and a free press were banned. Wealth, power, and land became concentrated under a small group of Díaz's supporters.

MINI BIO

BENITO JUÁREZ

Sculptures and busts of Juárez commemorate his lasting legacy to Mexico.

Benito Pablo Juárez García was born in Oaxaca, Mexico, on March 21, 1806. As a young adult, Juárez studied to become a lawyer. After graduating in 1831, he became involved in politics. He served as a state and federal legislator and later became governor of Oaxaca. Later he accepted the role of minister of justice. In this role, Juárez supported three major reforms in Mexico: land redistribution, a reduction of the Catholic Church's power in the government, and the passage of a new constitution. His leadership during the French occupation of Mexico held the nation together. Resistance by Juárez, along with international pressure, ultimately led France to withdraw its troops in 1867. After leaving office, Juárez continued to push for reforms in Mexico. He died of a heart attack in 1872.

> ### ZAPATA AND VILLA
>
> Two of the best-known figures of the Mexican Revolution are Emiliano Zapata and Francisco "Pancho" Villa. The men were leaders of the Revolution who were committed to the rights of the peasants. Their goal was to make sure the people who worked the land either owned it themselves or owned it as part of a group. Their trailblazing and often violent efforts pushed the revolution forward, and land was eventually redistributed to residents of the nation.

Seeking change, a wealthy businessman named Francisco Madero ran against Díaz for president in 1910. Díaz declared himself the winner and had Madero jailed. After Madero's release, he organized a revolt against Díaz. The revolt failed, but it ultimately led to the Mexican Revolution (1910–1920). This civil war claimed the lives of two million Mexicans before its end. It took years of rebuilding to bring prosperity and stability to Mexico. Mexicans elected Lázaro Cárdenas president in 1934, and he began to implement some of the reforms people had been seeking.

MODERN MEXICO

Under Cárdenas, Mexico returned to the ejido system, which redistributed land to peasants. The ejido system was an Indigenous method of community land ownership that had been practiced in Mexico for centuries. In this system, a community's land was divided among residents who each received a plot. By the 1960s, more than 154,440 square miles (400,000 sq km) of land that had once been owned by large estates had been redistributed.[8] Nearly half of all Mexicans received land in the ejido system.

The ejido system improved the lives of many peasants and small farmers. It also improved the economy and brought stability to the nation. In the years that followed, Mexican leaders continued to develop the nation. Some of the development involved modernizing the country's infrastructure. Workers built hydroelectric power plants and extended highways and railways. Other developments were social, such as extending voting rights to Mexican women. They received the right to vote in 1953, though the first election they could vote in was not until 1958.

In 1968, Mexico City hosted the Olympic Games. These were the first Olympic Games ever held in Latin America, and Mexico's government spent large amounts of money preparing for them. Local students thought the money should have been spent on social programs to develop Mexico instead. Ten days before the games, about 4,000 students protested in the capital's Plaza de las Tres Culturas. The protest turned violent when the military shot into the crowd, killing 200 unarmed protesters and injuring another 1,000.[9] The event was later known as the Tlatelolco Massacre.

During the 1970s, Mexico's economy grew quickly. The growth was paid for through loans the Mexican government took out from other countries. Officials planned to pay back the loans through profits from selling oil. But oil prices dropped sharply in the 1980s, and Mexico's government could not repay the loans. These problems were made worse by high unemployment rates and inflation.

Over the following decades, Mexico's economy gradually improved. The North American Free Trade Agreement (NAFTA), which went into effect in 1994, made trade easier between Mexico,

Mexico City hosted the Olympics in 1968, which was the first year that most of the events were broadcast in color. Mexico's athletes earned nine medals for the country.

the United States, and Canada. New factories built in Mexico provided jobs to many people, and the country's tourism industry boomed. And a new trade agreement—called the United States-Mexico-Canada Agreement (USMCA)—took effect on July 1, 2020. It set new rules for industrial and agricultural trade, and it also established new intellectual property protections among the three nations.

Even with the improvements and updated treaties, Mexico still faces many challenges. Drug cartels and violent crime plague the nation. Wealth inequality in the country remains, and poverty is a serious problem. The COVID-19 pandemic took many lives and slowed the economy's growth. Despite the challenges, Mexicans continue to work to improve their nation each day.

Left to right, Mexican president Enrique Peña Nieto, US president Donald Trump, and Canadian prime minister Justin Trudeau signed the USMCA at a ceremony in Argentina.

CHAPTER **FIVE**

PEOPLE AND CULTURE

Mexico is a melting pot of beliefs, cultures, languages, and values. Over the country's history, these widely varying elements have existed side by side, often influencing each other and blending with each other in surprising and unique ways. This has produced the vibrant culture and diverse population of modern Mexico.

Mexico is home to 129 million people, making it the tenth-most populous country in the world.[1] The country's population is quite young. About one-quarter of all Mexicans are under the age of 14. People have settled in various parts of Mexico throughout its history, but today a large portion of people live in or

The large, densely populated capital, Mexico City, is home to a diverse mix of cultures.

Lázaro Hernández Bautista is a renowned Nahuatl-language storyteller.

near large cities. Approximately 80 percent of Mexicans live in urban areas, the largest of which is Mexico City.[2]

The country has no official language. However, Spanish is the first language of approximately 95 percent of Mexicans.[3] It is the language spoken in public schools and in government proceedings. Mexico is home to the world's largest population of Spanish speakers, with more than twice as many Spanish speakers as Spain.

Though the constitution recognizes 68 Indigenous languages, a total of 143 native languages are spoken across Mexico.[4] Two of the most-spoken Indigenous languages are Mayan and the Aztec language called Nahuatl. About 1.5 million Mexicans can speak Nahuatl, and 750,000 speak Mayan.[5] Not all of Mexico's languages are spoken by such a large population, however. Language experts believe 60 of

Mexico's native languages are in danger of disappearing. For example, the language Kiliwa has only 36 remaining speakers.[6]

FOOD

Traditional foods in Mexico vary from region to region, but some are well loved and common throughout the country. One of the most common traditional ingredients used in Mexican cooking is corn. It is often dried and ground up into a flour called masa. Masa can be used to make one of Mexico's best-known foods: tortillas. They are a staple in Mexican meals and can be used in a variety of ways. Tortillas can serve as utensils to scoop food from a plate or bowl, they can be filled with meats and cheeses, or they can be fried and eaten as chips.

Chilies are also popular ingredients in Mexican cooking. They are used in a variety of ways to season food. Sometimes chilies are cooked into a sauce such as *mole* or *pipiáns* to add flavor and heat. Other times, the chilies may be diced and served fresh in salsas and relishes. In addition to chilies, Mexican cooks use a variety of herbs and spices in traditional foods. These include cinnamon,

FOODS FROM MEXICO

Many foods that are common in American diets are originally from Mexico. These foods include avocados, tomatoes, chilies, and vanilla. The cacao plant, which produces chocolate, is also native to Mexico. Maya and Aztecs used cacao to create a foamy drink that hot chocolate was later inspired by.

Tortillas are part of many Mexican dishes, and chefs in Mexican restaurants often prepare fresh tortillas in their kitchens.

cloves, cumin, thyme, and cilantro. Another common herb is epazote. It's an aromatic herb used to season beans, soups, stews, and sauces.

Mexican daily meals begin with breakfast, called *desayuno*. Common breakfast dishes include eggs and pan dulce, a sweet bread. The main meal of the day is lunch, which is called *comida* in Mexico. People eat this meal late in the afternoon, usually sometime between 2:00 and 4:30 p.m. Supper, which is called *cena*, is often served late in the evening. It's not uncommon to eat supper at 9:00. It is usually a light meal that can last late into the night.

A RICH, COMPLEX ETHNICITY

Mexican ethnicity springs from a blending of different peoples, values, and belief systems. Indigenous peoples of Mexico developed advanced civilizations with their own social structures and beliefs. After the Spanish conquered Mexico, the colonizers saw the Indigenous ways of life as inferior and actively suppressed them. Spanish values and culture replaced Indigenous ones in many parts of Mexico.

Spain's cultural dominance lasted for three centuries in Mexico. Despite this, Mexico's Indigenous cultures never completely disappeared. They intertwined with the Spanish culture, creating something entirely new. This cultural blending is often referred to as *mestizaje*, which means "racial mixing" in Spanish. Sixty-two percent of Mexicans identify as mestizo.[7] In the colonial era, this term referred specifically to someone's mixed race. Today it refers to people who consider themselves culturally Mexican.

Though they make up the majority of the population, mestizos are not the only ethnic group in Mexico. Roughly 15 percent of Mexicans—nearly 17 million people—identify as Indigenous.[8] This makes Mexico home to the largest population of Indigenous people in the Americas. One of the biggest challenges facing Mexico's Indigenous population is lack of recognition, including recognition of the legal rights of these peoples.

PLAZA DE LAS TRES CULTURAS

One of the places Mexico's rich heritage is publicly on display is at Mexico City's Plaza de las Tres Culturas ("Plaza of Three Cultures"). It represents Mexico's three major cultural periods: Indigenous, Spanish, and modern. The Indigenous culture is represented by the plaza's archaeological site of Tlatelolco, an Aztec city founded in 1338. Spanish culture is represented by a colonial-era school called El Colegio de Santa Cruz. Finally, the modern culture is represented by the plaza itself, which was designed by architect Mario Pani.

To improve the situation, the Mexican government signed the UN Declaration on the Rights of Indigenous Peoples in 2007. Despite this, the challenges for Mexico's Indigenous communities continue, especially regarding health care and human rights.

FAITH

The Indigenous cultures of Mexico have faith systems with their own gods and goddesses and ways of worshipping them. When the Spanish arrived in Mexico, they brought the Catholic religion, a branch of Christianity, with them. Spanish priests converted many Indigenous people, and by 2020 about 78 percent of Mexicans considered themselves Catholic. This made Mexico the world's second-largest Catholic country after Brazil. Another 11 percent of Mexicans were Protestant, and most of the remainder of the population did not follow any religion.[9]

The Catholic faith is woven very tightly into Mexico's daily life and culture. About half of Mexico's Catholics attend church weekly. Festivals throughout the year celebrate saints and holy days. Many of the celebrations are similar to what Catholics in other countries celebrate, such as Christmas and Easter. One celebration in Mexico honors the country's patron saint, the Virgin of Guadalupe, also called the Virgin Mary.

According to the Catholic faith, the Virgin Mary appeared to a newly converted Indigenous man named Juan Diego in 1531. The apparition occurred at Tepeyac Hill, an area just outside Mexico City. When Diego told the local bishop about his vision, the bishop demanded proof. The virgin reappeared to Diego and told him to return to Tepeyac Hill and gather what he found there.

Mexican Catholics carry an image of the Virgin Mary to the Basilica of Guadalupe to commemorate the feast day of the Virgin of Guadalupe.

When Diego returned, flowers covered the normally dry, rocky ground.

Diego gathered the flowers in his poncho, which was called a *tilma*, and returned to the bishop. As he opened his tilma, the flowers fell out on the floor and an image of the Virgin Mary appeared through them. Today, Diego's tilma is on display at the Basilica of Guadalupe, which stands near the site where the virgin appeared. It was the first time the Catholic Church recognized an appearance of the Virgin Mary in the Americas. Six million Mexicans make a pilgrimage to the basilica each year.[10]

JOINING BELIEFS

When Indigenous peoples converted to Catholicism, they often retained some of their traditions. Tepeyac Hill—the place where the Virgin Mary appeared to Juan Diego—had been a place where the Aztec people worshipped their fertility goddess, Tonantzin. Another example of this is in Mexico's Day of the Dead. Today, this festival celebrates the lives of departed family members, but it was not always this way. The festival has its roots in the Indigenous gods of the underworld and war, Mictlantecuhtli and Huitzilopochtli. Catholic priests united Indigenous worship of these gods with All Saints' Day, resulting in a uniquely Mexican festival that endures to this day.

ANCIENT ARTS

Mexico has a long history of amazing visual arts dating back to its earliest settlers. Some of Mexico's first artistic expressions came from the Olmec peoples. They carved massive heads from stone. Seventeen of these stone heads have been discovered. Historians believe they were carved between 1500 and 400 BCE. These stone faces are thought to be sculptures of Olmec rulers. The colossal carvings range from 4.8 to 11.2 feet (1.5 to

3.4 m) in height and weigh about eight short tons (7.3 metric tons).[11] The stone faces share a similar style, with full lips, broad cheeks, and flat noses. Most of the heads are adorned with helmets, which reflects what would have been worn in battle and during Olmec ball games.

Likewise, scientists have discovered traces of artistic expression from the height of the Mayan civilization. This includes temples, music, and poetry, as well as many murals. In 2009 in Calakmul, scientists uncovered murals that had been created sometime in the 600s CE. The artists used bright blue, green, yellow, red, and brown paints to create works of art on stone walls. The scenes often depicted figures engaged in chores of daily life, such as cooking food. The images were accompanied by hieroglyphics. Other murals uncovered depicted only warfare and royalty. The Calakmul murals provided a new window into daily life for common Maya people.

A jade mask created by the Maya was among the archaeological treasures found in Calakmul.

The Aztec civilization, too, produced a great variety of arts. They ranged from massive stone carvings to delicate pieces of jewelry. Religion and art were tightly connected for the Aztec people, and often their artwork depicted their gods. For religious ceremonies, artists produced elaborate clothing, such as shirts and headdresses, out of feathers. They also created ceremonial mosaic masks made from bits of coral, shell, and turquoise. Aztec temples often had elaborate carvings along the walls as well. Many works of Aztec art were destroyed during and after the Spanish conquest. Those that remain reveal the highly skilled artistry of the Aztec world.

MODERN ARTS

During Spanish control of Mexico, art largely matched the styles and tastes popular in Spain. Indigenous art had reflected religious themes and local rulers, and so did artwork under Spanish rule. From soaring, ornate cathedrals to the many portraits of the Virgin Mary, much of Mexico's colonial art was Catholic in nature. The art had its own regional influence too. For example, paintings from Mexico often featured Juan Diego with the Virgin Mary's image on his tilma. Other works of art, including paintings and statues, celebrated the local Spanish leaders who ruled the colony.

After the Mexican Revolution, the country's art began to change. It became less influenced by Spain and more influenced by local people. To unify the nation after the revolution, the government hired artists to paint murals in public buildings. The murals focused on the Mexican people and highlighted Indigenous values. They fostered a shared sense of history and bolstered

Large-scale paintings by Diego Rivera can be seen in Mexican museums.

65

pride in being Mexican. Of the muralists from this period, three became especially beloved. These three artists, known as *los tres grandes* ("the three greats"), were Diego Rivera, José Clemente Orozco, and David Alfaro Siqueiros. One of the most famous Mexican artists was painter Frida Kahlo. Born in 1907, she became well known for her self portraits. Kahlo's fame and reputation grew in the decades following her death in 1954.

In addition to visual arts, Mexico has a rich history of literature. Mexican author José Joaquín Fernández de Lizardi wrote *El Periquillo Sarniento* (*The Mangy Parrot*) in 1816. It is widely credited as the first novel written in Latin America. Mexico's Octavio Paz is considered one of Latin America's most famous poets. Paz published his first book in 1933 at the age of 19. His later writings often featured various images inspired by surrealism. Paz won the Nobel Prize in Literature in 1990. Other well-known Mexican authors include novelists Carlos Fuentes, Juan José Arreola, Juan Rulfo, Elena Poniatowska, and Amparo Dávila.

MINI BIO

ELENA PONIATOWSKA

Elena Poniatowska was born in France in 1933. Her mother was the daughter of Mexican aristocrats, and her father was a French count. In 1942, Poniatowska's family left France to escape World War II (1939–1945). They settled in Mexico City, where she began learning Spanish and going to school. In 1954, Poniatowska began her career as a journalist and later began writing novels as well. Perhaps her most famous book is called *La Noche de Tlatelolco* (*The Night of Tlatelolco*), which chronicled the 1968 Tlatelolco Massacre in Mexico City. In 2014, Poniatowska won the Cervantes Prize. It is the highest honor for an author writing in the Spanish language and is similar in honor to the Nobel Prize in Literature. Poniatowska was the first Mexican woman in history to win the Cervantes Prize.

Elena Poniatowska's works give voice to marginalized people.

CHAPTER **SIX**

POLITICS

Mexico's government is a federal republic made up of 32 states. A constitution that was approved in 1917 is the framework for Mexico's government. The country's federal government is organized into three branches: executive, legislative, and judicial. All three branches share equal power according to the constitution, but in practice this has not always happened. Until the late 1900s, the executive branch held more power than the others in determining how the country was run.

Mexican citizens vote for their representatives in the government. Mexico's president heads the executive branch and is elected to serve a six-year term, which is commonly referred to as the *sexenio*. Reelection to a second term is not permitted. The office of vice

The National Palace in Mexico City is the official residence of Mexico's president.

president does not exist in Mexico's executive branch. If the president were to die while in office, the legislative branch would select a temporary replacement until a special election could be held to elect a new president.

The president of Mexico has many duties and responsibilities. The president also acts as chief of state, head of government, and commander in chief of the military. The president's responsibilities include appointing federal court judges, ambassadors, cabinet members, and other high-level positions within the government. Issuing *reglamentos* is one of the president's jobs. Reglamentos are executive orders, which have the same effect as laws.

The legislative branch of Mexico's government is called the National Congress (Congreso de la Unión). It is split into two houses: the Senate (Cámara de Senadores) and the Chamber of Deputies (Cámara de Diputados). Mexican citizens elect 128 senators and 500 deputies to the National Congress.[1] Senators serve a six-year term, and deputies

THE CONSTITUTION OF 1917

Mexico's constitution was ratified on February 5, 1917, amid the turmoil of the Mexican Revolution. The leaders who drafted it had been greatly influenced by the revolution and the feelings of nationalism sweeping across Mexico, and the document reflects this. It remains one of the most progressive constitutions drafted in the 1900s. This document outlined a federal system of government and a bill of rights. It established separation of church and state, voting rights, and social welfare. It also called for any land that had been taken by the government illegally to be returned to its original owners. In the years since it was ratified, the constitution has been amended many times to reflect changes in Mexico.

> **ELECTING A PRESIDENT**
>
> Mexico holds its presidential elections every six years on the first Sunday in July. All Mexican citizens who are at least 18 years old and registered to vote may cast a ballot on election day. The Sunday following the election, official results are certified. The newly elected president takes office in December of the election year.

serve a three-year term. In the past, lawmakers could not be reelected to consecutive terms, but that changed in 2018. Now senators can serve two terms and deputies can serve four terms.

The role of the National Congress is to pass federal laws. To do this, members often form committees to study issues before proposing laws. Additional duties that fall to lawmakers are divided between the two houses. Members of the Senate approve presidential appointments. They also handle foreign-relations matters, such as approving or rejecting treaties and agreements with other nations. The Chamber of Deputies approves the federal budget and any public spending.

The judicial branch of Mexico's government is called the National Supreme Court of Justice (Suprema Corte de Justicia de la Nación). It interprets the nation's laws. The president appoints the court's 11 justices, who then must be approved by two-thirds of the Senate. Justices serve 15-year terms. According to Mexico's constitution, citizens have the right to a fair trial and humane treatment. In practice, this does not always happen, and the system often suffers from corruption, theft, and bribery.

State governments work in a similar way to the federal government. Each state has its own constitution with executive, legislative, and judicial branches. Governors head the executive

The Chamber of Deputies meets at the Legislative Palace of San Lázaro in Mexico City.

branch in each of the states, and they are elected to six-year terms. The legislative branch at the state level often has only one house, the Chamber of Deputies. Deputies in local governments serve for three-year terms. State courts interpret local laws and make up the judicial branch of each state. Below the state level of government are more than 2,000 municipalities, or municipios. These smaller administrative areas are headed by local elected officials.[2]

> Mexico's constitution has undergone frequent changes—in its first century, between 1917 and 2016, it was amended 227 times.[3]

TRANSPORTATION

One of the federal government's duties is to maintain the nation's various transportation systems. Mexico's varied landscape, vast size, and developing economy have made this a challenging job. The nation has a highway system that is heavily used to transport goods. However, the roadways are in poor condition in many places. The government has worked to upgrade and repair the roads, but its efforts have often not been enough to meet the demand of such a massive volume of drivers.

The Pan-American Highway also passes through Mexico. It is a network of highways that connects North America and South America. The massive highway project was first imagined in the 1920s to move goods relatively quickly and easily across the two continents. Today, the highway system covers 30,000 miles (48,000 km).[4] The section of the Pan-American Highway in Mexico was funded and built by the nation's federal government, though sections in other countries received US aid for construction.

In addition to highways, Mexico's transportation system includes other ways to travel. Mexico has a vast railway system. Railway lines have a hub in Mexico City, where they spread out across the nation to transport people and goods. The railways were originally owned and operated by the Mexican government, though today the system is operated by private companies. As tourism grew in Mexico, the government built many airports across the country. Much like the railways, Mexico's government originally owned the nation's two airlines, Aeroméxico and Mexicana. Today, these airlines are operated by private companies.

ARMED FORCES

The military is the part of the government that is responsible for the security of Mexico and its interests. Approximately 220,000 people serve in Mexico's armed forces, which includes the army, navy, and air force. The army is the largest arm of the military, with approximately 160,000 soldiers and officers.[5] The law makes military service compulsory for all males once they reach the age of 18. A lottery determines who is selected to serve. Those who are chosen must serve for one year. After that year, they are considered reserve soldiers until they reach age 40.

In 2019, Mexico's lawmakers voted in favor of amending the federal constitution to create a national guard. The national guard, which has approximately 100,000 members, was created as a civilian-controlled security force.[6] It was formed to aid federal police in cracking down on the violence that plagues Mexico. The goal was to free the military from doing police work. This did not work out as planned, however. Under pressure from the US government to stop undocumented immigration, about one-third of the national guard was sent to patrol the US-Mexico border. This focus on controlling migrants instead of fighting drug cartels angered those who live in border towns, such as Juárez, where crime rates have skyrocketed because of gangs and drug trafficking.

Under increasing pressure, Mexico's president made the national guard a formal part of the military in 2021. Today, security remains an important part of the military's job in Mexico. The nation is seeking new ways to use the military to address its problems. Mexico's military is now policing the nation's ports and performing customs inspections. Critics say that this is not the

Some members of Mexico's national guard patrol popular tourist areas.

solution to Mexico's crime problems, suggesting that instead the nation should be cleaning up corrupt police departments.

POLITICAL PARTIES

In the decades after the Mexican Revolution, the country's politics were dominated by a single political party: the Partido Revolucionario Institucional (PRI). Early on, the party's goal was to restore order and stability to Mexico after a decade of civil war. It was viewed as a populist party. Gradually the party's power grew, and it held a monopoly on the government. Each outgoing president handpicked his successor, which kept PRI's line of power unbroken.

During this time, the party grew corrupt. It silenced opposition and used bribery and fraud to ensure PRI-selected candidates won elections. During these years, the only party opposing PRI was called Partido Acción Nacional (PAN), though its candidates had few successes.

Mexico's government and PRI were connected so closely that they almost appeared to be one and the same. Discontentment with PRI grew, reaching a tipping point during the term of Carlos Salinas de Gortari. Salinas served as president from 1988 to 1994, and he faced scandal from the start. His election was secured following a computer error with vote counting that critics described as suspicious. During his term, drug trafficking grew to be a serious problem. His economic programs were unpopular with local businesses and farmers. In the state of Chiapas, a local army known as the Zapatistas revolted against the government.

CÁRDENAS AND PRD

Cuauhtémoc Cárdenas, the son of former PRI president Lázaro Cárdenas, launched a new political party in 1988. It was called the Partido de la Revolución Democrática (PRD). The party criticized policies of President Carlos Salinas de Gortari. In retaliation, approximately 500 activists connected with PRD were murdered between 1988 and 1994.[7] This did not stop Cárdenas or members of PRD. In 1997, he was elected mayor of Mexico City. It was the largest margin of victory for a party opposing PRI in Mexico's history.

Salinas's successor, PRI candidate Ernesto Zedillo, took over a country in turmoil. To address the concerns of the Mexican people, Zedillo reformed the election process. He created a new, independent electoral system that would be tried for the first time in the 2000 election. That year, PAN candidate Vicente Fox won the presidency. He was the first candidate to break PRI's 71-year victory streak. It was the country's first truly democratic election.

In the years since Fox's victory, Mexican political parties have grown in number. PRI and PAN are no longer the only options for voters. Two other parties have risen to power and popularity. They are the Partido de la Revolución Democrática (PRD) and Movimiento Regeneración Nacional (MORENA). With fairer elections and a greater variety of candidates to choose from, Mexico's political system has changed greatly.

Vicente Fox's 2000 presidential victory changed the Mexican political landscape.

CHAPTER **SEVEN**

ECONOMICS

Mexico has a $2.4-trillion economy.[1] This makes it the second-largest economy in Latin America, behind only Brazil. Mexico has one of the world's most open economies. It has free trade agreements with 50 countries across the globe. These agreements remove barriers to trade, such as tariffs and taxes. This has made Mexico the leading exporter in the region, with one-third of all goods exported from Latin America coming from Mexico.[2]

Many of the advances in Mexico's economy began in the 1990s. Some of the biggest changes happened under the leadership of Carlos Salinas de Gortari, who served as Mexico's president from 1988 to 1994. Salinas was committed to modernizing the economy and making free trade easier for Mexico's businesses.

A significant amount of Mexico's trade runs through the enormous port of Veracruz on the Gulf of Mexico.

One of the ways he did this was by selling some of Mexico's state-owned businesses to private owners. Under Salinas, Mexico's government sold 1,155 state-owned companies, accounting for 85 percent of the government's total business holdings.[3] He put the profits toward paying off the national debt.

Salinas also opened the economy to new, more open kinds of trade with other countries. One of the most sweeping changes was NAFTA. This agreement was signed by the leaders of North America's three largest countries—Mexico, the United States, and Canada—in 1992. NAFTA removed tariffs and other barriers to trade between the nations. The goal was to bring prosperity and new jobs to North America. NAFTA took effect in 1994 and remined in place until 2020.

NAFTA expanded Mexico's economy. Exports grew dramatically from $60 billion in 1994 to $400 billion in 2013.[4] But when the United States experienced a recession from 2007 to 2009, it also impacted Mexico's economy. American spending slowed during the recession, which in turn slowed demand for goods exported from Mexico. In the years since then, Mexico's economic growth has been steady but slow. Leaders of the United States,

THE PESO

Mexico's unit of currency is the peso. It is one of the oldest currencies in North America, and it was considered an official currency in Canada until 1854 and in the United States until 1857. This early form of the peso was considered so stable and secure that it served as the inspiration for early designs of US paper banknotes.

San Luis Potosí, a Mexican state, has sites that have been mined for gold and silver since the 1500s.

Canada, and Mexico did not renew NAFTA in 2020. Instead, they created a new trade agreement called the USMCA, which took effect on July 1, 2020.

NATURAL RESOURCES

For most of its history, Mexico's citizens have relied on their country's vast natural resources to form the backbone of the economy. Some of the most important resources were found in the country's many mines. Mining for metals brought wealth and jobs to Mexico for centuries. Multiple Latin American nations are rich in silver. Together, Mexico, Bolivia, and Peru produced 85 percent of the world's silver between 1500 and 1800.[5] Today, Mexico remains the world's leading producer of silver. Mexican mines also supply other resources, including sulfur, zinc, lead, and copper.

Oil is another one of Mexico's valuable natural resources. Mexico began oil production in 1901. By 1920, Mexico was the world leader in oil exports. New oil reserves were discovered in Mexico in the 1970s. In 1972, scientists built huge oil wells in the states of Chiapas and Campeche. Two years later, additional oil wells were added in Veracruz, Baja California Norte, Chiapas, and Tabasco. Oil production ramped up, and Mexico soon began to produce more than the nation could consume. Mexico began to export an increasing amount of oil. Between 1977 and 1982, oil exports increased from 400 million barrels to 1.1 billion barrels per year.[6]

In 2020, Mexico produced 1.9 million barrels of oil a day. This made it the fourth-largest oil producer in the Americas after the United States, Canada, and Brazil.[7] For decades, a company called Petróleos Mexicanos (Pemex) controlled the country's oil industry. Mexico's government owned Pemex. It had a monopoly on the oil industry, and

ROLE OF THE CONSTITUTION

Ownership of natural resources lay at the heart of the creation of Pemex. Article 27 of Mexico's 1917 Constitution states, "Ownership of the lands and waters within the boundaries of the national territory is vested originally in the Nation."[8] Originally, Article 27 was meant to handle land reforms after the Mexican Revolution. But in 1938, President Lázaro Cárdenas used it as justification for expelling any foreign companies from Mexico's oil industry and creating the government-owned Pemex. In Cárdenas's view, the oil was a natural resource that belonged to the people of Mexico, not foreign businesses.

Cancún, located on the Yucatán Peninsula, features a long string of beachside resorts.

its profits funded a large part of the federal budget for many years. Under Mexico's president Enrique Peña Nieto, reforms opened Mexico's oil industry to foreign competition in 2014.

Mexico has other natural resources as well. The coastal waters off Mexico teem with marine life that sustains commercial fishing. Waters off the Gulf Coast are good for catching shrimp, marlins, and billfish. The Pacific Coast is rich in sardines, anchovies, and tuna. The country's many forests are another natural resource. Tropical forests of the Yucatán Peninsula are the source of wood such as mahogany, cedar, and rosewood. The tropical forests also have sapodilla trees, which produce chicle. It is a kind of latex used to make chewing gum.

MEXICO'S INDUSTRIES

Traditionally, Mexico's economy was based on agriculture. That began to change gradually starting in the 1940s, and today the service industry makes up the largest part of Mexico's economy. It accounts for approximately 60 percent of the nation's gross domestic product (GDP), or the total value of the goods and services the country produces in a year.[9] Workers in this sector provide a wide variety of services rather than making products to sell. Hotels, restaurants, shops, and trade make up a large portion of the service economy.

Much of Mexico's service economy is centered on tourism. Mexico is the top foreign vacation spot for US tourists. Jobs connected with the tourism industry employ 2.3 million Mexicans.[10] The country's world-class beaches and resorts, ancient ruins, and modern cities draw millions of tourists each year. One of its most popular tourist destinations is Tulum. Located on the Yucatán Peninsula, Tulum boasts well-preserved Maya ruins along the sparkling blue waters of the Caribbean Sea. Other popular beach vacation spots in Mexico include Playa del Carmen, Cancún, and Cozumel.

Manufacturing is another important part of Mexico's economy. Historically, the country's manufacturing plants were in and around Mexico City. This area provided the workforce and resources to make production easier. Manufacturing in Mexico began to change in the 1960s with

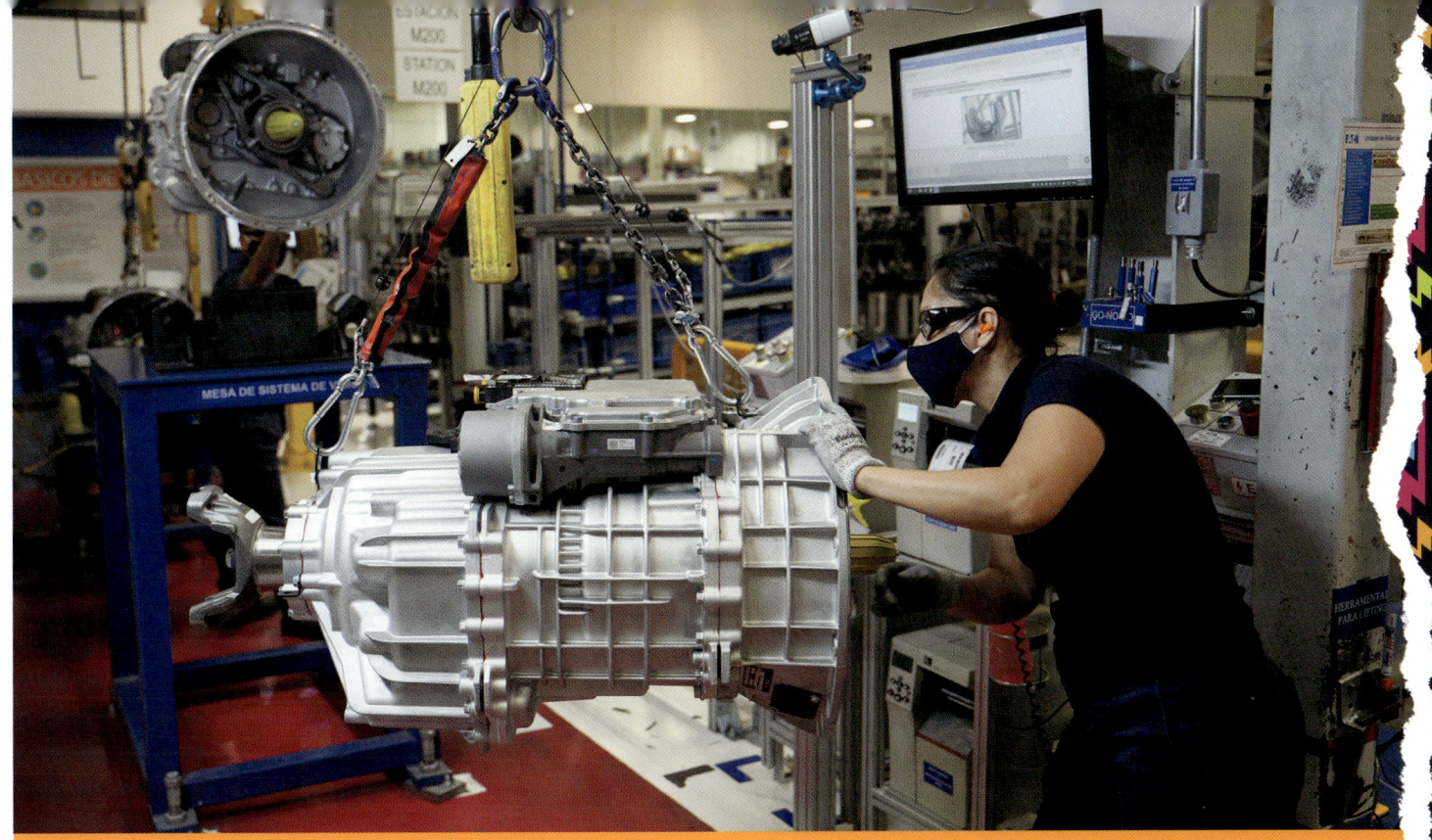

Manufacturing workers put new safety measures, such as requiring face masks, into place during the COVID-19 pandemic.

the creation of maquiladoras. These plants imported parts without paying any trade fees, such as tariffs. Workers at the maquiladoras then assembled the parts into a wide variety of products. The completed products were then exported. The lower cost of wages in Mexico made this system beneficial to foreign businesses, and new maquiladoras began to pop up in border towns between the United States and Mexico.

Today, manufacturing makes up approximately 30 percent of Mexico's GDP.[11] Businesses from the United States and Canada set up manufacturing plants in Mexico. They are drawn to the country's low manufacturing costs, large labor pool, and skilled workers. People who work in Mexico's plants manufacture a wide variety of products. Automotive, aerospace, medical-device, and clothing manufacturing make up the largest part of this sector of the economy.

Agriculture is a small but important part of Mexico's economy, making up less than 5 percent of the nation's GDP.[12] Along the Gulf Coast and the highlands of Chiapas, farmers grow sugarcane and a variety of fruits such as bananas, pineapples, and papayas. This part of the country is also good for growing cacao, vanilla, and coffee. Coffee is Mexico's most valuable export crop. The land near Mexico's Mesa Central is considered the country's breadbasket, and farmers there grow wheat, corn, and many types of vegetables. The production of cotton and livestock, especially cattle, is also an important part of Mexico's agricultural industry.

> The wealthiest 10 percent of Mexican citizens hold 43 percent of the nation's income. The poorest 10 percent of Mexican citizens hold less than 2 percent.[13]

A DEVELOPING ECONOMY

Mexico has what economists describe as a developing economy. In this kind of economy, workers often receive low wages. They may have to spend their entire earnings to survive, so they have little in the way of savings. Not everyone in a developing economy struggles financially, though. Often the wealth in a developing economy is spread out unevenly. A wide gap exists between a small, elite group with tremendous wealth and a much larger group of people with little money.

While a small, growing middle class exists in Mexico's largest cities, it is not common across the country. Approximately 40 percent of Mexico's population lives below the poverty line.[14] Earning less than the equivalent of $111 per month in rural areas and less than $170 per month in urban areas was considered living below the poverty line in Mexico in 2021. People in these categories do not have enough money to pay for basic food, housing, and health care.

As a result of this, remittances have become a growing part of Mexico's economy. A remittance is money sent from one person to another. Family members who live and work in the United States often send money back to relatives living in Mexico. In 2021, the remittances sent to Mexico totaled $51.6 billion, which was a historic high.

There are more than 500,000 coffee producers in Mexico. More than half work on small farms, and more than 80 percent are Indigenous farmers.

This made Mexico the third-largest receiver of remittances, behind China and India. Remittances make up nearly 4 percent of Mexico's GDP, which is nearly equal to the amount of money agriculture adds to the nation's GDP.[15]

Remittances became an even more important source of income during the COVID-19 pandemic. The average income in Mexico fell by 7 percent in 2020.[16] The decline hit hardest in parts of Mexico that relied on income from tourists. This was felt especially hard in the southern part of the country. In August 2021, President Andrés Manuel López Obrador pledged to provide government help by raising the minimum wage and increasing aid for the elderly. Even with measures such as these, reversing the economic effects of the COVID-19 pandemic could take many years.

REMITTANCES

The average monthly remittance received in Mexican homes in 2021 was $340. This money was often spent on basic goods and services, such as food, clothing, and health care. Often the remittances end up in some of Mexico's most violence-prone states, such as Guanajuato, Zacatecas, Jalisco, and Michoacán. It can create dangerous situations. "Families in Michoacán are trying to hide that they are receiving remittances," said Agustín Escobar Latapí, a professor at Mexico's Center for Research and Higher Studies in Social Anthropology. "They try to go to a bank branch that isn't near their house, and not show it off, because these families become a target for kidnappings, to get the money."[17]

For those living in poverty, remittances can be a vital lifeline.

CHAPTER EIGHT

MEXICO TODAY

Modern Mexico reflects the country's Indigenous and Spanish heritages, resulting in an entirely new and dynamic culture. Despite this, the country is anything but uniform. Mexico encompasses a large land area, and each region has its own foods, festivals, and music. Likewise, the sizable gaps between the poor and the wealthy and between the urban and the rural have created cultural differences. These differences have resulted in not one Mexico, but many. It is a nation of varied experiences, viewpoints, and values.

Despite stereotypes of the Mexican pace of life being slow, relaxed, and laid-back, this is not reality for

Celebrations of Mexican culture sometimes feature parades, dancing, and music.

A modern quinceañera is often an elaborate party featuring formal clothes.

most modern families. As in the United States and Canada, the days of most Mexicans are filled with daily commutes, work, school, and family obligations. A typical day might begin with a light breakfast of pan dulce and juice or coffee. Then it's off to work or school for the day.

Public schools in Mexico are free, and attendance is required by law from ages six to 15. Elementary school is called *primaria*, middle school is called *secundaria*, and high school is called *prepa*. Some young people, most commonly those who have money and resources, continue their studies after prepa at a university or technical school. Others stop school after prepa and begin working.

Family is a high priority for most Mexicans, and daily life is often built around it. In Mexico it's common for several generations to live under the same roof, sharing household responsibilities such as caring for children, shopping, cooking, and paying bills. Families are often united around special events, such as birthdays and graduations. Religious rites—such as baptism, first communion, confirmation, and marriage—also bring Mexican families together to celebrate.

Another important event in Mexican family life is a girl's quinceañera. It is a special celebration that happens when a girl turns 15. It is considered her transition from being a girl to being a woman. The quinceañera usually begins with a church mass. The birthday girl often wears a long, formal dress and a tiara for the occasion and has several friends by her side as attendants. After the mass, the family throws a party to celebrate. It often involves gifts, food, music, and dancing.

Likewise, weddings can be large, joyous affairs. Under Mexican law, a couple is not legally married without a civil service. Many people complete this service first. It is usually a small ceremony at a *registro civil*, which is a government office. Couples typically then have a second wedding ceremony at a church. The reception that follows is often a large party filled with traditions such *baile de billete*. As the bride and groom dance around the room, guests pin money to them as a gift.

CHANGING ATTITUDES

Many of the values related to family remain traditional and rooted in Mexico's overwhelmingly Catholic faith. That does not mean the country has not adopted new attitudes, though. In 2010, Mexico City legalized same-sex marriages, and several states followed its lead in the next decade. Legal acceptance has not always meant cultural acceptance. Violence and discrimination against people in the LGBTQ community remain high in many parts of the country.

HAVING FUN

Listening to music and dancing are some of the most popular ways to relax and have fun in Mexico. Mexico has many different styles of traditional music. One of the best-known styles is called mariachi. It is usually performed by a band that plays traditional stringed instruments, such as a *vihuela*, a *guitarrón*, and a *guittara de golpe*. These instruments are joined by a bass guitar, violins, and trumpets. The songs mariachi bands play are diverse—ballads, folk dances, and even polkas are part of a typical playlist.

Another popular form of entertainment in Mexico is watching sports. Soccer, which is called *fútbol* in Spanish, is the most popular sport in Mexico. Massive crowds flock to stadiums to watch the 18 teams in Mexico's top professional division, Liga MX. The league's two most popular teams are Club América and Club Deportivo Guadalajara. Fans eagerly anticipate each match between the two rivals, which is referred to as El Super Clásico. In addition to watching soccer, many young people in Mexico also enjoy playing it themselves.

Soccer isn't the only popular sport in Mexico. Many people enjoy watching *lucha libre*, which is

BIRTHPLACE OF MEXICAN SOCCER

Soccer is a part of Mexican culture that runs deep, but it started from an unlikely source. English miners working in the city of Pachuca brought the game to Mexico. The miners played their first match in 1889. Today, Pachuca is considered the birthplace of Mexican soccer. It is home to the University of Soccer and Sports Sciences, the Soccer Hall of Fame, and its own professional team: Club de Fútbol Pachuca, which plays in Liga MX.

Mexico's lucha libre form of professional wrestling has proven highly influential, gaining popularity among wrestling fans in other countries.

a form of professional wrestling. It is equal parts theater and sport, with wrestlers often donning masks and outrageous costumes. Boxing is another much-loved sport in Mexico, and the country has produced many world-class fighters. Arguably the most famous is Julio César Chávez. He won five world titles and had 87 consecutive wins after turning pro in 1980.[1]

Historically, bullfighting has been a popular sport in Mexico. It originated in Spain, and colonists introduced it to Mexico when they arrived. People still watch bullfights in Mexico today, often as part of local festivals. Though still popular, this sport has seen a decline in recent years. Supporters of animal welfare have raised ethical questions about bullfighting, and it has been banned in the states of Sonora, Guerrero, and Coahuila.

Mexican forces have captured many high-level members of drug cartels, and the country is still working to reduce violent crime.

CHALLENGES

While Mexicans have created an amazing and vibrant culture, the country still faces many problems. One of the most recent challenges has been the COVID-19 pandemic, which first swept across the globe in early 2020. Mexico, which relies heavily on tourism, never closed its border during the pandemic. Testing and vaccinations were slow to be implemented in many parts of the country. As a result of this situation, Mexico became a COVID-19 hotspot and one of the hardest-hit countries in the world. Mexico ranked fifth in the world in the number of deaths caused by COVID-19 by July 2022.[2]

In addition to COVID-19, Mexico faces two other major challenges: violence and poverty. Violence in Mexico is often related to drug cartels. After taking office in 2006, President Felipe Calderón took a new approach to fighting the violence. He replaced local police officers with soldiers. Rather than curb violence, however, under this plan the number of murders quadrupled from 3,000 in 2007 to 12,000 in 2009. Calderón's successor, Enrique Peña Nieto, changed little when he took office, and 2017 marked Mexico's highest recorded death toll. That year alone, more than 25,000 people were murdered in Mexico.[3]

These figures do not tell the whole story, though. The fight against the drug cartels has had several successes. Mexican authorities have seized large amounts of drugs and weapons. Several leaders of drug cartels have been imprisoned. And corruption within Mexico's justice system is slowly being addressed. The problem is complex, however, and the fight against drug cartels and violent crimes is far from over.

> **Ninety-seven percent of all Mexican immigrants move to the United States. More than half of Mexico's immigrants to the United States live in Texas and California.[5]**

Having more than 40 percent of the population living under the poverty line is another challenge in Mexico.[4] When President Andrés Manuel López Obrador took office in 2018, he did so with a promise to make the needs of the poor a high priority. Before he could get much traction, however, the COVID-19 pandemic hit. Budget cuts, business shutdowns, job losses, and a general downturn in Mexico's economy made an already-difficult situation worse for many Mexicans struggling to make ends meet.

A desire to escape poverty and violence has motivated some Mexicans to leave their country. Many want to start a new life in the United States. In 2021, US authorities had 1.6 million encounters with migrants on the border. It was the highest number on record and more than quadruple the encounters in the year before. More than a quarter of these encounters involved people attempting to cross multiple times.[6] Mexico was the most common home country among migrants attempting to cross the border, though migrants traveling from elsewhere in Latin America are also included in these numbers.

Migrants attempting to enter the country without US authorization or documentation often face one of two scenarios. They may be immediately sent back to their home countries. Or they may be temporarily detained by US authorities. And in some cases, children are arriving at the border

PUSH AND PULL FACTORS

When a person decides to immigrate, push and pull factors have a large influence. Push factors are what motivate a person to leave a country. High crime rates and widespread poverty are examples of push factors. Pull factors are what attract an immigrant to a specific new country. Better jobs, health care, and schools are pull factors. Another powerful pull factor is having relatives already living in the country. They can provide support for newly arrived immigrants. Push and pull factors have had a large influence on the number of Mexicans who have chosen to immigrate to the United States in the past several decades.

unaccompanied by adults, which complicates the situation. This large-scale migration has caused a crisis at the US-Mexico border, which critics contend is worsened by the aggressive enforcement policies of US immigration authorities. Leaders from the United States and Mexico are working to address the crisis.

While the challenges facing Mexico are large, its people remain proud of their nation and hopeful about its future. The nation's land is rich in natural resources, the government is changing and becoming less corrupt, and the economy rebounded after the COVID-19 crisis. Throughout the nation's history, its people have adapted their ways of life, beliefs, and culture as the nation changed. The result is a modern Mexican culture that is bright and vibrant. Today, that spirit of hope and resilience remains alive in Mexico's people as they face the future.

People are working to tackle Mexico's modern challenges while appreciating the country's natural beauty, rich history, and diverse cultures.

ESSENTIAL FACTS

OFFICIAL NAME: UNITED MEXICAN STATES

GEOGRAPHY

Area: 758,449 square miles (1,964,375 sq km)

Highest Elevation: Citlaltépetl Volcano at 18,490 feet (5,636 m)

Lowest Elevation: Laguna Salada at −33 feet (−10 m)

PEOPLE

Population: 129.2 million (2022 est.)

Most Populous City: Mexico City (22.09 million)

Ethnic Groups: Mostly Mestizo; also Amerindian and minority other

Religions: Christianity (mostly Catholicism, also Protestantism) and unaffiliated

GOVERNMENT

Type of Government: Federal presidential republic

Capital: Mexico City

Head of State and Government: President

Legislature: Bicameral, with a Cámara de Senadores and Cámara de Diputados

ECONOMY

Currency: Peso

Major Industries: Agriculture, food and beverage production, tobacco, chemicals, iron and steel, mining, textiles, clothing, motor vehicles, tourism

Natural Resources: Petroleum, silver, antimony, copper, gold, lead, zinc, natural gas, timber

NATIONAL SYMBOLS

National Anthem: "Himno Nacional Mexicana" ("Mexican National Anthem")

National Bird: Crested caracara

National Flower: Dahlia

GLOSSARY

CARTEL
A group of people in the same business who fix prices and limit competition.

COMPULSORY
Required by law.

DORMANT
Temporarily inactive.

HIEROGLYPH
A picture representing a word or sound.

INDIGENOUS
Relating to the earliest people living in a place.

INFLATION
An increase in the price of goods and services.

NATIONALISM
A belief in one's own nation above all others.

PATRON SAINT
A saint who is said to protect a specific place, activity, person, or thing.

PEDICAB
A small, pedal-operated vehicle that serves as a taxi.

PILGRIMAGE
A journey to a sacred place to show devotion.

POROUS
Having many holes or pores.

RICHTER SCALE
A numerical scale to measure the strength of an earthquake.

SURREALISM
An artistic and literary movement that combines images of reality with images of fantasy.

TARIFF
A set of prices, fees, duties, or taxes on imported or exported goods.

TECTONIC PLATE
A huge piece of rock that makes up Earth's crust and upper mantle.

ADDITIONAL RESOURCES

SELECTED BIBLIOGRAPHY

Bernstein, Marvin David, et al. "Mexico." *Encyclopedia Britannica*, 29 Apr. 2022, britannica.com. Accessed 29 Apr. 2022.

Maddicks, Russell. *Mexico: The Essential Guide to Customs & Culture*. Kuperard, 2017.

Suchlicki, Jaime. *Mexico: From Montezuma to the Rise of the PAN*. Potomac, 2008.

FURTHER READINGS

Carser, A. R. *US Immigration Policy*. Abdo, 2018.

Nardo, Don. *Cause & Effect: The Ancient Aztecs*. ReferencePoint, 2018.

Sheen, Barbara. *Growing Up in Mexico*. ReferencePoint, 2018.

ONLINE RESOURCES

To learn more about Mexico, please visit **abdobooklinks.com** or scan this QR code. These links are routinely monitored and updated to provide the most current information available.

MORE INFORMATION

For more information on this subject, contact or visit the following organizations:

Mexican Cultural Institute
2829 16th St. NW
Washington, DC 20009
instituteofmexicodc.org/index.php/contact/
The Mexican Cultural Institute shares Mexican culture in the United States through a variety of programs, art, and community events.

National Museum of Anthropology
Av. Paseo de la Reforma y Calzada Gandhi s/n Col. Chapultepec, Polanco
Del. Miguel Hidalgo, C.P. 11560
Mexico City, Mexico
mna.inah.gob.mx
The National Museum of Anthropology is Mexico's largest museum and features a massive collection of artifacts from throughout Mexican history.

National Museum of Mexican Art
1852 W. 19th St.
Chicago, IL 60608
nationalmuseumofmexicanart.org
The National Museum of Mexican Art displays a collection of 18,000 pieces of art created throughout Mexico's long history, making it one of the largest collections of Mexican art in the United States.

SOURCE NOTES

CHAPTER 1. A TOUR OF MEXICO

1. "Mexico." *CIA World Factbook*, 5 July 2022, cia.gov. Accessed 12 July 2022.
2. "Tenochtitlán." *Encyclopedia Britannica*, 29 Aug. 2019, britannica.com. Accessed 12 July 2022.
3. Mark Cartwright. "Coyolxauhqui." *Encyclopedia of World History*, 11 Feb. 2016, worldhistory.org. Accessed 12 July 2022.
4. Eva Maria Weininger. "Mexico, Third Place among the Most Visited Countries in 2020." *WMP Mexico Advisors*, 22 Jan. 2021, wmp.mx. Accessed 12 July 2022.

CHAPTER 2. GEOGRAPHY

1. "Mexico." *CIA World Factbook*, 5 July 2022, cia.gov. Accessed 12 July 2022.
2. Marvin David Bernstein et al. "Mexico." *Encyclopedia Britannica*, 8 July 2022, britannica.com. Accessed 12 July 2022.
3. Donald Dilworth Brand. "Rio Grande." *Encyclopedia Britannica*, 20 Nov. 2019, britannica.com. Accessed 12 July 2022.
4. "Chihuahuan Desert Ecoregion." *National Park Service*, 20 Jan. 2022, nps.gov. Accessed 12 July 2022.
5. "Chihuahuan Desert." *World Wildlife Fund*, 2022, worldwildlife.org. Accessed 12 July 2022.
6. "Copper Canyon Tours." *Copper Canyon*, 2022, coppercanyon.com. Accessed 12 July 2022.
7. Carlos Lazcano. "A Descent to Measure the Basaseachi Waterfall in Chihuahua." *México Desconocido*, n.d., mexicodesconocido.com.mx. Accessed 22 July 2022.
8. "Baja California." *Encyclopedia Britannica*, 7 May 2019, britannica.com. Accessed 12 July 2022.
9. L. O'Hanlon. "The Looming Crisis of Sinking Ground in Mexico City." *Eos*, 22 Apr. 2021, eos.org. Accessed 12 July 2022.
10. "Yucatán Peninsula." *Encyclopedia Britannica*, 7 Aug. 2008, britannica.com. Accessed 12 July 2022.
11. Brendan Sainsbury. *Mexico*. Lonely Planet, 2018. 843.
12. "Sistema Sac Aktun—Longest Underwater Cave." *Karst Geochemistry and Hydrogeology*, n.d., sites.northwestern.edu. Accessed 12 July 2022.
13. "Mexico Volcanoes." *Smithsonian Institution Global Volcanism Program*, 2013, volcano.si.edu. Accessed 12 July 2022.
14. "The Ring of Fire." *National Geographic*, n.d., nationalgeographic.com. Accessed 12 July 2022.
15. Luke Waterson. *Insight Guides: Mexico*. APA Publications, 2019. 78–79.
16. Karina Suárez. "Mexican Earthquake's Proximity to Guerrero Seismic Gap Causes Alarm." *El País*, 10 Sept. 2021, english.elpais.com. Accessed 12 July 2022.
17. "The Eruption of Paricutin (1943–1952)." *San Diego State University*, n.d., sci.sdsu.edu. Accessed 22 July 2022.
18. "Mexico City Earthquake of 1985." *Encyclopedia Britannica*, 21 Sept. 2021, britannica.com. Accessed 12 July 2022.
19. "2017 Mexico Earthquakes: Facts, FAQs, and How to Help." *World Vision*, 21 Sept. 2017, worldvision.org. Accessed 12 July 2022.

CHAPTER 3. PLANTS AND ANIMALS
1. "Chihuahuan Desert Ecoregion." *National Park Service*, 20 Jan. 2022, nps.gov. Accessed 12 July 2022.
2. "Creosote Bush." *DesertUSA*, n.d., desertusa.com. Accessed 22 July 2022.
3. "Larrea Tridentata." *USDA Fire Effects Information System*, n.d., fs.fed.us. Accessed 12 July 2022.
4. "Chihuahuan Desert Ecoregion," *National Park Service*.
5. "Greater Roadrunner." *White Sands National Park*, 21 Aug. 2020, nps.gov. Accessed 12 July 2022.
6. "Mexico Has the Most Cacti in the World." *El Universal*, 21 Sept. 2018, eluniversal.com.mx. Accessed 12 July 2022.
7. Chad P. Dawson and John C. Hendee. *Introduction to Forests and Renewable Resources*. Waveland Press, 2012. 65–68.
8. "Bosques Templados." *Biodiversidad Mexicana*, n.d., biodiversidad.gob.mx. Accessed 12 July 2022.
9. "Bosques Templados," *Biodiversidad Mexicana*.
10. Brendan Sainsbury. *Mexico*. Lonely Planet, 2018. 624–625.
11. "Resplendent Quetzal." *National Geographic*, n.d., nationalgeographic.com. Accessed 12 July 2022.
12. "Selvas Secas." *Biodiversidad Mexicana*, n.d., biodiversidad.gob.mx. Accessed 12 July 2022.
13. "Selvas Húmedas." *Biodiversidad Mexicana*, n.d., biodiversidad.gob.mx. Accessed 12 July 2022.
14. "Selvas Húmedas," *Biodiversidad Mexicana*.
15. "Giant Kelp." *Oceana*, n.d., oceana.org. Accessed 12 July 2022.
16. "Mesoamerican Reef." *World Wildlife Fund*, n.d., worldwildlife.org. Accessed 12 July 2022.

CHAPTER 4. HISTORY
1. "Teotihuacán." *Encyclopedia Britannica*, 29 Sept. 2021, britannica.com. Accessed 12 July 2022.
2. Manuel Aguilar-Moreno. "Ulama: The Pre-Columbian Ballgame Survives Today." *American Indian Magazine*, 2016, americanindianmagazine.org. Accessed 12 July 2022.
3. "Aztec." *Encyclopedia Britannica*, 12 Aug. 2021, britannica.com. Accessed 12 July 2022.
4. "Aztec," *Encyclopedia Britannica*.
5. Brendan Sainsbury. *Mexico*. Lonely Planet, 2018. 816–817.
6. Sainsbury, *Mexico*, 819.
7. "Mexican-American War." *Encyclopedia Britannica*, 21 June 2021, britannica.com. Accessed 12 July 2022.
8. Sainsbury, *Mexico*, 816–817.
9. "Mexico City 1968 Olympic Games." *Encyclopedia Britannica*, 5 Oct. 2021, britannica.com. Accessed 12 July 2022.

SOURCE NOTES CONTINUED

CHAPTER 5. PEOPLE AND CULTURE

1. "Mexico." *CIA World Factbook*, 5 July 2022, cia.gov. Accessed 12 July 2022.
2. "Urban Population – Mexico." *World Bank*, 2022, data.worldbank.org. Accessed 12 July 2022.
3. Russell Maddicks. *Mexico: The Essential Guide to Customs & Culture*. Kuperard, 2017. 152–155.
4. Christine Dell'Amore. "Sixty Languages at Risk of Extinction in Mexico." *National Geographic*, 12 Apr. 2014, nationalgeographic.com. Accessed 12 July 2022.
5. Maddicks, *Mexico*, 152–155.
6. Dell'Amore, "Sixty Languages at Risk of Extinction in Mexico," *National Geographic*.
7. "Mexico," *CIA World Factbook*.
8. "Indigenous People in Mexico." *IWGIA*, n.d., iwgia.org. Accessed 12 July 2022.
9. "2020 Report on International Religious Freedom: Mexico." *US Department of State*, 12 May 2021, state.gov. Accessed 12 July 2022.
10. Luke Waterson. *Insight Guides: Mexico*. APA Publications, 2019. 22.
11. "Olmec Colossal Heads: What Are They?" *Gaia*, 26 Feb. 2020, gaia.com. Accessed 12 July 2022.

CHAPTER 6. POLITICS

1. "Mexico." *CIA World Factbook*, 5 July 2022, cia.gov. Accessed 12 July 2022.
2. Marvin David Bernstein et al. "Mexico." *Encyclopedia Britannica*, 12 Nov. 2021, britannica.com. Accessed 12 July 2022.
3. Rivera León and Maura Arturo. "Understanding Constitutional Amendments in Mexico." *Mexican Law Review*, 2017, sciencedirect.com. Accessed 12 July 2022.
4. Melissa Petruzzello. "Pan-American Highway." *Encyclopedia Britannica*, 24 June 2022, britannica.com. Accessed 12 July 2022.
5. "Mexico," *CIA World Factbook*.
6. "Mexico," *CIA World Factbook*.
7. "Cuauhtémoc Cárdenas." *Encyclopedia Britannica*, 27 Apr. 2021, britannica.com. Accessed 12 July 2022.

CHAPTER 7. ECONOMICS

1. "Mexico." *CIA World Factbook*, 5 July 2022, cia.gov. Accessed 12 July 2022.
2. "Overview of the Mexican Economy." *Mexican Embassy of the Philippines*, n.d., embamex.sre.gob.mx. Accessed 12 July 2022.
3. Jaime Suchlicki. *Mexico: From the Montezuma to the Rise of the PAN*. Potomac Books, 2008. 145.
4. Peter Bondarenko. "North American Free Trade Agreement." *Encyclopedia Britannica*, 12 Nov. 2020, britannica.com. Accessed 12 July 2022.
5. "Silver Mining in History." *Silver Institute*, n.d., silverinstitute.org. Accessed 12 July 2022.
6. "Mexico: A Country Study." *US Library of Congress*, n.d., countrystudies.us. Accessed 12 July 2022.
7. "Oil and Gas." *International Trade Administration*, 2 Sept. 2021, trade.gov. Accessed 12 July 2022.
8. "Mexico's Constitution of 1917 with Amendments through 2015." *Constitute*, n.d., constituteproject.org. Accessed 12 July 2022.
9. "Mexico," *CIA World Factbook*.
10. "Mexico: Tourism." *OECD iLibrary*, 2022, oecd-ilibrary.org. Accessed 12 July 2022.
11. "Mexico," *CIA World Factbook*.
12. "Mexico," *CIA World Factbook*.
13. Vanessa Rubio. "This Isn't the Path to Solving Mexico's Inequality." *Americas Quarterly*, 21 Oct. 2020, americasquarterly.org. Accessed 12 July 2022.
14. Russell Maddicks. *Mexico: The Essential Guide to Customs & Culture*. Kuperard, 2017. 48.
15. "Mexico's Remittances Surged 27% in 2021 to $51.6 Billion." *AP News*, 1 Feb. 2022, apnews.com. Accessed 12 July 2022.
16. "Poverty Increases in Mexico amid COVID-19 Pandemic." *AP News*, 5 Aug. 2021, apnews.com. Accessed 12 July 2022.
17. Mark Stevenson. "Mexico's Remittances Pass $50 Billion, Surge during Pandemic." *US News and World Report*, 26 Jan. 2022, usnews.com. Accessed 12 July 2022.

CHAPTER 8. MEXICO TODAY

1. Brendan Sainsbury. *Mexico*. Lonely Planet, 2018. 825–826.
2. "Mortality Analyses." *Johns Hopkins Coronavirus Resource Center*, 22 July 2022, coronavirus.jhu.edu. Accessed 22 July 2022.
3. Luke Waterson. *Insight Guides: Mexico*. APA Publications, 2019. 73.
4. "Ranks of Mexican Poor Swell to Reach Nearly Half the Population." *Reuters*, 5 Aug. 2021, reuters.com. Accessed 12 July 2022.
5. Emma Israel and Jeanne Batalova. "Mexican Immigrants in the United States." *Migration Policy Institute*, 5 Nov. 2020, migrationpolicy.org. Accessed 12 July 2022.
6. John Gramlich and Alissa Scheller. "What's Happening at the US–Mexico Border in 7 Charts." *Pew Research Center*, 9 Nov. 2021, pewresearch.org. Accessed 12 July 2022.

INDEX

agriculture, 19, 52, 84, 86, 88
Aztecs, 7–10, 12, 31, 41, 42–43, 56, 57, 59, 62, 64

Baja California, 18, 26, 37, 82
birds, 29, 30–31, 33

cactuses, 9, 28, 29, 42
Cárdenas, Lázaro, 49, 76, 82
Caribbean Sea, 14, 17, 21, 22, 37, 84
Catedral Metropolitana, 12
Catholicism, 44, 48, 60–62, 64, 93
cenotes, 22
Chichén Itzá, 41
Chihuahuan Desert, 18, 26–28
constitution, 56, 68, 70, 71, 72, 74, 82
Copper Canyon, 17, 18
Cortés, Hernán, 43
COVID-19 pandemic, 13, 52, 88, 96–97, 99
Coyolxauhqui Stone, 9
creosote bush, 26–28
currency, 80

dancing, 10, 93, 94
deforestation, 33
Díaz, Porfirio, 47, 49
Diego, Juan, 60, 62
drug cartels, 52, 74, 76, 97

earthquakes, 12, 21, 24–25
education, 92
ejido system, 49–50
El Bajío, 19
ethnic groups, 58–59

food, 10, 57–58
forests, 30–31, 33, 83–84
Fox, Vicente, 77

Gulf of Mexico, 14, 16, 17, 21

Hidalgo, Miguel, 6, 45

Indigenous peoples, 41, 42–43, 44, 49, 56, 58–60, 64

Juárez, Benito, 47, 48
jungles, 32–33

Kahlo, Frida, 66
kelp, 37

Lake Texcoco, 21, 42
languages, 56–57
López Obrador, Andrés Manuel, 88, 97

Madero, Francisco, 49
mammals, 29, 30
mangrove forests, 34
manufacturing industry, 84–86
Maya, 22, 31, 41, 42, 56, 57, 63–64, 84
Mesoamerican Reef, 37
Mexican Plateau, 16
Mexican-American War, 45–47
Mexico City, 4–13, 17, 20–21, 25, 40, 42, 50, 56, 60, 62, 67, 73, 76, 84, 93
migrants, 74, 97, 98
military, 50, 70, 74
monarch butterfly, 30
Montezuma II, 43
music, 10, 63, 90, 93, 94

National Congress, 70–71
national guard, 74
National Supreme Court of
    Justice, 71
natural resources, 19, 81–84
North American Free Trade
    Agreement (NAFTA), 50, 80–81
Nueva España, 44–45

oil, 50, 82–83
Olmec, 38–40, 62–63
Olympic Games, 50

Pacific Ocean, 14, 17, 22, 24,
    37, 83
Pan-American Highway, 73
Parque Alameda Central, 12, 13
Paz, Octavio, 66
political parties, 75–77
pollution, 21
Poniatowska, Elena, 66, 67
poverty, 52, 87, 97–98
president, 6, 47, 49, 68–71, 74, 76,
    78, 82, 83, 88, 97
professional wrestling, 94–95

quetzals, 31
quinceañeras, 93

religions, 60–62
remittances, 87–88
reptiles, 28
Ring of Fire, 22–25
Río Bravo del Norte, 14
Rivera, Diego, 7, 66

Salinas de Gortari, Carlos, 76,
    78–80
service industry, 84
Sierra Madre, 16, 18, 30
soccer, 94
Spain, 6, 12, 44–45, 47, 56, 59,
    64, 95
state governments, 71–72

Templo Mayor, 8–9, 13
Tenochtitlán, 8–9, 42–44
Teotihuacano people, 40
tourism, 10, 12, 13, 22, 52, 73, 84,
    88, 96
transportation, 73

ulama, 41
United States, 14, 18, 30, 45–46,
    52, 80, 82, 85, 86, 87, 92, 97,
    98–99
United States-Mexico-Canada
    Agreement (USMCA), 52, 81

volcanoes, 22, 24

Yucatán Peninsula, 21–22, 32, 37,
    41, 84

Zedillo, Ernesto, 77
Zócalo, 6, 8, 10, 12

ABOUT THE AUTHOR

KATE CONLEY

Kate Conley has been writing nonfiction books for children for more than ten years. When she's not writing, Conley spends her time reading, sewing, and solving crossword puzzles. She lives in Minnesota with her husband and two children.